Mike Suman

ISBN 9780615488288
Library of Congress Control Number: 2011929568
Subject headings:
    Business
    Self Help

Author contact information

Web: www.mikesuman.com

Please understand we cannot help everyone with their project so please refrain from contacting us for advice. Thanks, Mike

Should Your Idea Become a Business?

Editor - Alan Rosas

6206 Sweet Clover Lane, Caledonia, MI 49316

All wood product components used in the manufacturing of this book in Tennessee or Pennsylvania are Sustainable Forestry Initiative® (SFI®) Certified Sourcing. All wood product components used in the Milton Keynes UK Production Center are Forest Stewardship Council™ (FSC®) Mixed Credit. FSC® C084699

Acknowledgements

For years, when I read the acknowledgement sections in a book, I wondered how some authors could thank so many people. After all, how many people does it take to write a book? Now I know.

I can't begin to thank everyone by name, but to all of you who read manuscripts and took the time to give me your feedback, thank you so much. It is a lot to ask.

To all of the bosses I had over the years, I thank you for giving me enough rope to hang myself and the patience to let me wander and grow – I know it was not always easy.

To all of the teammates I worked with over the years, I thank you because I learned something from each one of you and had fun 99% of the time.

To Makenzie, Hunter, Wade, and MC – When you have a dream (and you will) give it some time. If you move forward with a concept and someone says they do not like it – please remember they are responding to the idea. It's not about you! It could be they are right. It could be they don't get it, or it even could be about them.

How you sort though all the feedback says more about your capabilities than creating the opportunity in the first place.

The most important thing to remember is, the only way to never be judged is to never get in a position to be judged. The only way to accomplish that is to never take a risk – and trust me that is not any of you.

Stay positive, have fun and keep moving forward!

About the Cover

My goal is to discuss the things that are the "between the lines" issues when it comes to individuals trying to start a new business based on an idea, working alone or inside a company.

We have all heard the saying, "That is the 800 pound Gorilla in the room," referring to a subject that is important but, for some reason, cannot be discussed openly.

There are some points in this book that are more important than others – they can't all be critical. Occasionally you will see one or more baby Gorillas next to a subject. These symbols draw your attention to a specific point, and the more gorillas, the more important the point. I thought it would be more fun than using asterisks with foot notes.

Plus, it gave me an excuse to use the cover picture "Perplexed Gorilla" by photographer Ron Reznick, www.digital-images.net. — because, some days, that's how we all feel when trying to figure out what to do with an idea that could be great if we only knew what to do next

Table of Contents

Background

Over the years, I have been blessed to be part of many great product development teams. Together we have created, launched and managed fantastic new products that many people use every day. We also created businesses around those products that kept our enterprises thriving and responsive to world markets.

We all start the same way — by being the "new person." In my case, I climbed the corporate ladder to become the Vice President of Marketing and Business Development in a private company that we grew from 20 million to almost one billion in annual sales.

That was a stepping stone to an even more challenging position at a large, public company (over 20 billion in annual sales) as a Group Vice President in charge New Business Development, Public Relations, IT, Marketing, and Advance Sales.

Interestingly, the same methods that have worked for me in large corporations have been successful as I have developed my own products on a smaller scale. My products have sold on QVC, my own web sites, through wholesale distributors, and on online sales channels like eBay — and still do on a daily basis. It is a kick to wake up and see what sold overnight around the world.

In recent years, I have been called upon to speak to college classes, angel investors and venture capital groups. I have been asked to participate on college advisory boards and local inventor network boards. I enjoy working with people who are passionate about their ideas and I mentor new inventors whenever I can.

Part of my business also involves consulting in a wide variety of industries. Usually, the company is missing projected goals in growth or profit. Sometimes they want fresh product ideas or they ask for help because their R&D investment has failed to produce the sales they had planned.

I also work with individuals who are tired of working for others and wondering what it might be like to do their own thing for their next life chapter.

Getting started, I would like you to think about three questions.

Are you an Inventor?

Are you good at thinking of new solutions that improve the way things are done? Are the ideas and solutions you develop recognized as "new and novel" by peers in their industries?

Are you an Innovator?

Can you transform a new idea from a concept into a product or service that will create demand in the market place?

Are you an Entrepreneur?

Do you have a good understanding of business management practices including all aspects of operations, balance sheet control, and team building?

The truth is that very few of us are excellent at all three of these functions. My goal with these questions is to get you to consider that these are three different activities, each requiring different skill sets. I want you to stop thinking that you are developing a new product and start understanding what you really need to do is create a business based on your idea.

No matter which of these functions you identify with most, please be thinking about these three questions as you read this book and which one(s) fit your strengths best. When you recognize your strengths, it becomes obvious in what areas you need some support.

When someone comes to me with an idea and asks what I think, I seldom evaluate the idea; instead I try to quickly estimate their ability to create a business around their idea. At this point, it is not only about the idea; it is about the ability to do what it takes to find out if there is a market. This is true if they work alone and need to sell the idea to the world or if they work inside a corporation and must sell it to peers and management.

Whether I work with individuals or with corporations, I always get asked one question that I never answer. Without fail, they ask if I think their idea is a good one. I do not answer for one simple reason:

Even if one critic does not like your idea, there are about seven billion people in the world. Even if 98% of them do not like your product, that still leaves a potential market pool of 140 million people. Who am I to discourage a product that might appeal to 140 million people? If you have a way to target your market, you should go ahead with testing and validating your business idea no matter what critics say.

The questions I do answer have taken the form of this book. Over the years of consulting, inventing and marketing, I have accumulated a powerful list of tips, tools, and tests.

Not long ago a friend of mine suggested I formalize what I've learned into a book. What a journey that has been. Regardless of the success of this book I will be forever grateful to her for that suggestion and support.

The chart in Figure 1 has blank fields representing the many skill areas in which you will need support to bring your idea to life and make it into a business.

By the end of this book, we will have these blank fields filled in with resources, tips, and tools that I have developed and used over the years.

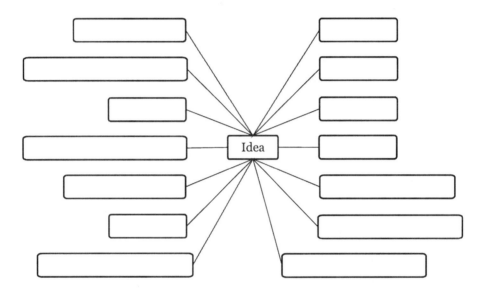

Figure 1

A second reason for including this chart with empty fields is to give you a sense for the scale of what it takes to create a business around your idea. Building a functioning business structure can be daunting, but when done with planning, can be just as rewarding and important as the idea itself.

Why Read This Book?

What It's Not - This is not a "how to" book. It will not tell you how to develop a product, sell it and get rich. This is a distillation of the things I have found to be effective while developing products and businesses over my lifetime.

What It Is - This book has been written for the new inventor working independently *and* for the person in business development teams working for companies large and small. The opportunities and struggles for both can be very similar. Both have to sell their ideas to someone else to make things happen.

Many of the companies for which I consult have excellent written processes that spell out exactly what their employees need to do to ideate, package, and propose new product ideas.

The inventors that work alone in their garages also have access to good processes using any of the countless books on "how to" create new products, write business plans, and develop marketing strategies.

And yet, at times, both independent and corporate inventors, innovators, and entrepreneurs can use support and a compass to help guide them. It is my hope that this book serves that function for both groups, public and private.

This book is also intended to:

1. Help you determine if your idea should be a business and if you are up to the task.
2. To serve as a good tool to test your idea before you spend more than minimally needed, to find out.
3. Serve as a guide to help you avoid some of the common mistakes made by private innovators and companies.

The last chapter is a resource for anyone leading business development teams as a manager who needs to inspire, encourage and guide their inventors, innovators, and start up teams. As you read the last chapter please think about how your leadership style encourages the people creating the future of your company.

So, What Message is this Economy Sending Us?

The financial mess we have been in the last few years is a huge wakeup call. We need to strengthen the kind of atmosphere that allows us to invent, innovate, and launch more new concepts than ever in our history. We can accomplish that by embracing risk, failing fast, and placing more (but smaller) bets on more creative ideas than ever.

You will see that, for a business book, this volume has a casual style and some measure of humor and storytelling. I believe stories are a great way to share, so I have included several short case histories to illustrate things that worked well and some things that did not go so well. They were all learning experiences.

Life is too short to take things too seriously, and odds are, we are going to be on this earth only once (at least in our current form). Therefore, I hope you get to work on things you are passionate about. Have as much fun as possible in your life's journey. If this book and sharing the experiences of my business development life can bring you a little of that – all is well!

Enjoy the book and we will see you at the back cover.

Have fun and Good Luck!

Some Basic Truths

About Teams

The truth is that most inventors are more comfortable in their own space than in the boardroom. As long as you recognize your weaknesses, you can look for help and build a team. I have never launched anything without a solid team.

Without hesitation, it takes a variety of talent to get a new business going. Nobody does it alone, unless you have the ability to be – simultaneously - an engineer, designer, finance guru, marketing genius, salesperson, manufacturing expert and CEO. You will find the skills of a hard-working and diverse team behind virtually every successful business concept or product launch.

I just filed for my fiftieth patent — again with the help of a great team. In the beginning, you might not have the budget to build an ideal team, so you might wear several hats. But you can't do it all and you should plan on team-building as part of your product development.

With a few exceptions, I currently rent support for almost everything I do. These paid supporters are still a part of my business family. When I have a tax question I call my CPA. Yes he charges me but he knows more about taxes than I do. More importantly, I recognized that I needed that help in the first place.

About Market Demand

I can't begin to guess how many great products never get off the shelf. On the other hand, we all have watched questionable products do really well. It may seem that there is no rhyme or reason to success, but there is one good predictor that must never be ignored. The litmus test is market demand, tested via the distribution system – a test you conduct *before* you invest your life savings or your company's treasure. Sometimes the market isn't ready or isn't interested.

When that happens, put on the brakes and start with another idea or bring an earlier idea back to life when the market is ready. Also, you cannot take a lack of market interest personally. Many products do not get traction for three to five years after development. Sometimes you have to let the market come to you.

About Courage

Whether the market tells you to move forward or not, congratulate yourself for getting off the couch and giving it a shot. Most people don't even try.

The truth is most new businesses based on new products fail to ever make money. So think about building your business process as the foundation of your company and then drop in your product ideas, because ideas can come and go but a strong business model can adapt to any product.

I am not saying you need more than one product to have a successful business. I am suggesting that if you spend the time to build a business model around your idea and if your product does not make it, you could still have a great model that you can simply plug more ideas into over and over again.

About Successful Products

It seems to me that the makeup of a successful product or business concept is 25% idea, 25% execution, 25% timing, and 25% luck. Of course, hard work and due diligence in your process can greatly influence the luck part. I don't have a problem with being more lucky than good.

About Embracing Risk

One huge reason that I love doing what I do is the sense of adventure. There is no guarantee of success when you start a new business based on a new product or service. As long as you keep your investment risk low so you won't lose the house or get fired for betting your companies budget on a long shot– it can be exciting and rewarding.

Every day, the phone could ring and change my life. That is a real kick, even if the phone doesn't ring – it is a great way to live your life.

I understand the risks and, trust me, I am not blind to the long odds of any new product or business idea hitting the big time. But just the possibility of getting a "big-win phone call" about two or three opportunities you have on the table is a great thing to have in the back of your mind. It creates a positive outlook on life and others will be asking you why you always seem to be so optimistic.

Most people that lend money to businesses have excellent risk screening tools to make sure, if you fail, they get most of their investment back. Most lenders have one goal in mind – they will lend you money when there is an acceptable risk.

There have been several TV shows with inventors pitching their ideas to so-called experts in an attempt to raise money. These shows drive me nuts. The experts ask inventors if they have competition, do they have a patent, do they have sales, has anyone tried to buy your company, what are you going to do with the money and on and on. All good questions, but if any inventor could answer all those questions in a way that would give the lender incentive to loan money, they would not need the money.

Plus, some of the offers are crazy. I remember one episode in which the inventor had sales of one million dollars with no debt and a promise from a well-known global company to buy another million dollars of product. The inventor was asking for a cash flow loan of $50,000 for inventory management.

The person making the loan said they would loan the inventor $50,000 in return for 50% of their company plus interest on the loan.

This highlights the first rule of borrowing — **make sure you need it.**

About Tolerating Chaos

Some people cannot handle the unknown and are unsettled until things are in a neat, organized box, which, of course, never happens with an untried idea. How will you handle the unknown? Without question, the biggest variable when it comes to creating new products and new business is you.

You can find all sorts of personality measurement tools that can help you understand your strengths, but in the end, if you want a life of predictability and cannot handle chaos, you might want to give this chaotic adventure a second thought. However if you are a great idea person and a good manager with excellent delegation skills, you can find team members to deal with the chaotic things while you play to your strengths.

The chaos is not even the largest challenge. It's time. Be prepared to invest more time than you have for anything you have done before. If it takes a great deal more time that you planned, the "adventure" can be suffocating for you and everyone around you.

About Research Sources

Some of the advice and tools I have included might not make sense for your specific business so focus on the most relevant ideas and regard the rest as context. Also, you will see I suggest some web sites to help you do research and analyze businesses and opportunities. I am not paid by any of the resources I mention. They are simply ones I know to be effective. If you have favorite sites that provide the same services, please use your own sources. There are more popping up every day.

About Selling an Idea Without Starting a Business

If you simply want to sell your idea with no involvement other than a royalty, upfront payment, or commission that is just fine. It happens all the time.

Even with such a limited approach you will still need to do most of the things I am going to suggest in this book. The more clearly you can demonstrate value, the more money you can expect for your idea. Everyone you approach to sell your idea will put together their own risk scenario with or without you. So why not give them *your* version?

Demonstrating Evidence of Value

Anyone who might buy your idea or become an investor will need to see evidence of value in your business. Here are 10 tools you can use to create the value story you will need to sell your idea in the market or inside the company you work for. We will get into all of these in detail later in this book, but this gives you a resource page to work from.

1. Your Customer's Problem - see Pain Points - page 65

2. The Solution Story - see Prescriptive Selling - page 61

3. The Sales Plan - see Sell with Evidence, Not Just Hype – page 73

4. Distribution Plan - see No Distribution Plan - page 30

5. The Competitive Landscape - see Creating a Competitive Matrix - page 51 and Customer Value Matrix - page 67

6. Patent Status - see A Few Thoughts About Patent Protection - page 38

7. Market Test Results - see Consumer Market Testing - page 40

8. Risks - see What the Heck is a Business FMEA? - page 90

9. Something about you - see O Yeah? What About You? - on page 103

10. Business Case Metrics – As stated in other areas in this book I do not discuss how to write a business plan. If you are in a corporation I am sure you have a written process you are expected to follow. If your company does not have a process or you work alone you can go to the library or any book store and buy several good books that will show you how to build and follow a business plan.

⚑ Red Flags ⚑

Whenever I see new business innovators taking any of these all-too-common steps, I get concerned that they could be headed for trouble. These are my "red flag" issues. My goal for this red flag section is to expose you to the pitfalls that trip up many inventors, innovators and entrepreneurs. Look over this list and raise your attention level a little if and when you work in these areas. These red flag issues are not in any order because the ones that apply will vary by industry and product — and if you are on your own or in a company.

⚑ #1 Faith in Inventors' Support Services

Don't be too quick to sign up with commercial inventors' support services. If step one or two is to get you to send them money – be careful! Ask them for a list of people you can call that are happy customers along with a list of unhappy customers so you can get the story from both sides. If they tell you they have no unhappy customers – walk away. If they tell you they do not give out that information – run away.

I suggest you do a Google search with their name and the word "fraud" and see what you get. To get more information on scams that pray on inventors go to US Government site on inventor fraud at http://www.inventorfraud.com/pto.pdf

⚑ #2 No Evidence of a Market 🐵🐵

Don't spend a lot of money on a patent before there is evidence of a market. Distribution can be much more important than the idea itself. If someone comes to me with a great idea for a new product I say, "Good for you and good luck!" If a distributor comes to me with a need in the market that he is convinced will sell, I say, "how can I help!"

I know of many more ideas gathering dust on the shelf because of no distribution than I know of distributors who have a product need that remains unfulfilled. If at all possible I suggest you start with the market need and work back to the idea.

⚑#3 Not Doing Due Diligence 🙈🙉🙊

1. Do existing market search — find out if your idea is already in the market or if it was in the market and failed.

2. Do a patent deep dive — using patent search tools also as business search tools.

3. Find and test a distribution system.

We will be getting into more on these issues later.

⚑#4 Undefined Partnerships 🙈 🙈

Don't take on partners that do not contribute obvious value and always have a written exit plan for all parties before the relationship starts. Yep, sounds a lot like a prenuptial agreement because it is. In the beginning of any partnership (in marriage or in business) it can be awkward to discuss what happens if there is a split. However, you simply must do this because, as the old saying goes, "a partnership is the only ship that might never sail." Of course, we need partnerships, but make sure they are put together professionally with as many "what ifs" as reasonable.

I have been asked to work with a few companies that are having partnership trouble. When I ask each person, privately, to tell me why they got together in the first place, when they say, "we were friends," that almost always is a danger sign. Sure, like-mindedness is more fun in the beginning, but, if possible, partners should not duplicate each other's strengths.

We have all heard the saying, "opposites attract in a marriage" – for which I have no input. But for a business, you need the skills of opposites to make things go. If partners happen to be friends, great, but don't make friendship the lone reason to partner.

⚑ #5 Borrowing Too Early and Too Much 🐵🐵

Don't borrow money when the market has not been established because, if there is no market you don't need money. Let me say that another way. Why would you borrow money if you have not done everything you can to find out if the business is going to make it? Pay as you go (bootstrapping) is the best way to get started if you possibly can.

On the other side, if you have orders for a well-protected part, you should not need to take on debt other than for cash flow to support sales. I have refused orders because the customer would not give me some sort of upfront payment. If you think it sounds strange to ask for a percentage up front with a custom order, just do business with the Chinese. Many Chinese businesses ask for total payment with the order.

⚑ #6 Speaking of Chinese

Be very careful when you start working with suppliers offshore. I am not anti-import, but you must make sure you understand the risks. I have worked with many offshore businesses over the years and most uphold the highest standards of ethical behavior. However, business philosophies vary with culture and you need to make sure the culture of the people with whom you work has been considered when looking for suppliers and partners.

First of all, regardless of where you live, there is no choice but to buy and sell globally. There are clear economic reasons to do so. For example, if you have a ten dollar retail product that costs four dollars to make in the U.S., and the four dollar cost makes profit impossible, you do not keep going. If you can manufacture the same product offshore for two dollars, and that works with your profit plan, you can generate a value of eight dollars, and perhaps you can move forward with the offshore strategy.

My point is, if you did not import, there would be no added value to the US economy. If you do import, it will add eight dollars. Therefore, it is good for our economy if you import. I am sure there are economists who would disagree with my simplified view of creating value for our economy. However, some of those same experts are now having trouble forecasting the future because every time they look ahead, they get a glimpse of their past performance (which is sometimes not so accurate).

Also, I import things that are not available here, like bamboo. It is fine to either stay domestic or import, but my first choice is to consider the value added to my country and go from there.

When considering offshore suppliers, inventors have to watch out for patent infringement. Also, the minimum quantity required by the offshore manufacturer might be more than you will sell in ten years. Plus, if you have a quality problem, it can be difficult to get support from an offshore manufacturer — unless you have a local as a team member.

I believe Americans work as hard or harder than any culture in the world. We work hard to support our high standard of living and that cost keeps going up. But hard work doesn't level the playing field. Foreign competition can be unfair when countries manipulate their currencies, impose punishing duties or provide subsidies to industries such as steel, autos, motorcycles, meat, energy, and on and on. Some foreign companies employ workers that may be underpaid, without benefits, are underage or work in hazardous environments. Even so, factory working conditions are a step-up from subsistence farming and there is no shortage of willing workers.

My recommendation is; do not try to beat the Chinese at being Chinese, because they are really good at it. The key consideration is the cost of hand labor. When you start your design, you are also determining what percentage of sales you will need to cover the cost of labor.

When the first lines are being drawn for your product, you need to design the level of automation versus hand labor. If you want to keep labor down as a percentage of sales, you can add in some automated processes, but remember to put that equipment investment in your business plan. Balance the cost of automation equipment against the risks and delays incurred if you must use inexpensive offshore hand labor.

Whether your design requires lots of labor or not, make sure what you do is represented in your plan. The worst case scenario is that you are surprised when you get knocked off by an offshore competitor and you did not have a plan in your BFMEA (Business Failure Mode Effect Analysis). More on this later.

There is no foolproof way to buy parts offshore. Trust me, it is a nightmare to have sold orders waiting for parts from China and fifteen days into your thirty-day shipment deadline, your engineers call and say they found a mistake and those parts are no good. Can you say 747 air shipments?

Many big box stores will tell you that they will only buy from you if you get your parts from China. Ask them if they are willing to take the risk of managing all of that and you will get a resounding no! The risk is all yours and, if you do not have an agent on the ground in China – be very careful.

The truth is, there is no single way of managing the global supply issue. I prefer to take a little less margin (until I can prove there is a solid market), using domestic suppliers. When volumes go up, then I can sit down with my suppliers and decide whether to add automation, go off shore, or a combination. But I have not risked my new operation by rolling the dice on a container load of parts somewhere in the pacific. Surf's up!

⚑ #7 Borrowing Money from Friends and Family 🐵🐵

Of course it is okay to borrow money from family and friends when both parties agree to a defined need. But don't be quick to borrow from relatives or friends for a new idea start up unless, of course, you want to add some spice to your family reunions. If you have a rich uncle that has so much money he does not care if you lose his money, then get all you can and send me some. Or maybe you should do whatever he did to get it and not take the loan in the first place.

The only time any loan feels good is when you have the completed payment book in your hand. When you borrow from family or friends for a new idea, even if you pay back the money with interest, sometimes there is "loan hangover" which can create feelings "if it weren't for me," you can never pay back. Just be careful and if you borrow money from family for a new idea, have it professionally constructed like a bank note.

⚑ # 8 Spending Too Much at Startup 🐵🐵🐵

Don't spend initial money on items that are not essential at the beginning of a project — for example, don't lease an office when working at home or in a borrowed space will do for a while. In the beginning, fight fixed cost as much as possible. This is true if you are on your own or working inside a company. It is all money you might not need to spend if the idea does not prove out.

⚑ # 9 Ignoring Feature Creep

Keep the business plan dynamic and keep costs updated as changes are made. When a new idea is launched, it always involves some level of continuous improvement. Left unchecked, this can lead to something I call "feature creep." It is important to remember that each improvement affects costs and your business plan should record each change. Ignore feature creep and you damage profits before you get started.

You will know you have a good finance person when they seem almost happy to point out that you gave away your profit when you made the last "feature creep" changes. They are not really happy. Your finance person just feels good about finding the hole in the boat before you sank. Unfortunately, most finance people do not offer a solution when they point out that your business plan now has more balls in the air than the Chinese National Ping Pong Championship.

Make your adjustments, hug your finance person, say thanks and go back to work. A worse scenario is to find a big money leak after a year of production.

#10 Signing Ill-Advised Lease Contracts

I have watched this happen over and over. New startup leaders become so excited, they don't think twice about signing a long term lease for space without having exit clauses. It comes back to haunt them every time.

If they are successful and need more space, they can't get out of the lease. If their business fails, they also can't get out. They find themselves being forced into the real estate business to sublet their space or pay for a multi-year, early exit.

It is worth the money to have an attorney that specializes in lease agreements take a look at your contract before you sign. Yep it will cost a few hundred dollars but could save you thousands.

⚑#11 Protecting Your Dream 🙈

Don't share your dreams for this venture with everyone you know. Keep the progress of your ideas as private as you can for as long as you can. I have watched inventors keep pushing projects long after they failed just to keep from telling people. They feel like failures — especially if they borrowed money from the people they do not want to tell. As my Dad used to say "boy when you find yourself in a hole the first thing to do is put the shovel down".

⚑#12 FIRE Ready AIM

Over the years, I have found almost any idea or action plan gets clearer with a little incubation time. I keep a simple, three by five card file that I use as a Big Idea aging vault. I put ideas in the vault (even though it is just a plastic recipe box) and forget about them for as long as I can. Then I pull them out and decide if they are still good ideas.

I toss out at least half and the rest I leave for more aging. A few of the ideas get put together in a plan to start some level of development. Instant action, for me, is not usually a good thing. Take some time and let your ideas mature a little. Some industrial designers call this "ideation incubation."

I also keep a sketch pad by my bed. I wake up and scribble notes and even do sketches or I can't get back to sleep. But I must admit, most of my middle-of-the-night-ideas don't seem to work that well in daylight, but, they seemed really brilliant at 3:00 am!

⚑ #13 What About Using Cyberspace to Distribute?

Maybe you're thinking you can use web distribution to cut out those greedy middlemen! Absolutely true, and I do it all the time. But please be aware that selling directly to consumers (B2C) or to other businesses (B2B) also takes a lot of effort, time, and in some cases, just as much money.

The power of using a master distributor can be amazing. If you sell 100,000 parts to a distributor, it is one decision for you to sell 100,000 parts. If you sell 100,000 parts, one at a time on the Internet, it is 100,000 decisions. You need to spend time and money convincing thousands of people to buy.

I do sell on the Internet and it works great. I also sell on eBay, to retailers, wholesalers, direct to other businesses and on my own websites.

Each channel has advantages and disadvantages. The most important thing to remember about direct selling via the Internet is that the system is changing constantly. It will continue to do so forever. Can anyone say that the last and final method to find customers and sell on the Internet has been found – of course not!

Using an Internet distribution system alone will and does work, but it is not a passive venture. It will require continual self-education and weekly, if not daily direct involvement. Yes, you can hire support services to do that for you, and that is a great alternative.

However, please remember those services that find your site and start calling with promises to get your hits up higher than you ever dreamed – will accept none of your risk for their service.

They have a great business model when they can sell you search words, have it not work, and have it be your fault. Great work if you can get it.

⚑ #14 Working With the Mother Ship

Selling on eBay is fairly easy and cheap to set up. I found a local expert to coach me and I was up and running in a couple of hours and she charged me only fifty dollars. Plus, it was fun to sit at a local coffee shop and watch my first product go live. However, be sure to understand the commissions eBay charges can be high (up to 15% commission for one of my current products), plus the credit card charges, and shipping. Prepaid shipping made a huge difference on eBay for me as far as increased sales.

So be sure you include all your costs when setting pricing. Set the online price high enough to cover eBay charges while still leaving margin room for your distributor when you need one later.

⚑ #15 Getting your Own Credit Card System

Setting up a traditional credit card system (sometimes known as a merchant account or gateway) drove me to tears at least twice. Even though PayPal costs more, for me it was worth it. Setting up your own charge card system takes a ton of time and involves at least three organizations that, at times, do not seem to want to work together: banks, clearing houses, and finally the card company itself.

I sell merchandise every day using PayPal and it works well. Their website does not explain clearly (in my opinion) that PayPal takes other credit cards, but they do. So, on my websites I state clearly that a PayPal account is not necessary for regular credit card use.

⚐ #16 Buying Ad Words Without a Plan

As soon as you get your Internet site up and running, you will start to get calls from companies that promise that they can greatly improve your sales by selling you search words. I must say that buying search words has not worked all that well for me yet. Maybe I am the only one, but I seem to pay $600 a month for the words and my sales seem to go up about that same amount — if I am lucky.

You will get many offers that claim they can work miracles with your hits (and I am sure some can) but it can get real expensive real fast. Some "Search Engine Optimization" companies want to charge you thousands per month. And of course, please pay up front. If you use these services, make sure you have a no-penalty divorce clause. If you want to get them nervous, ask them to take the risk with you. If they are so convinced that your hits and sales will go up, ask them if you can pay them only after successful results. I can tell you what will happen. It is called a dial tone in your ear.

Of course, things like "pay per click" can make a difference. But I suggest you go slow, test, and direct your funding toward what is working. But keep testing and measuring and be ready to shift when things change, because they will.

⚐ #17 Channel Conflict 🐵🐵🐵

There are many forms of channel conflict. Most conflicts develop when someone in the distribution chain is selling a product for a lower retail price than the wholesale price paid by distributors. This would be like a car company selling their cars online for less than the price the dealer needs to make a profit – and then expecting the dealers to do the service for free.

Some cell phone companies do exactly this, and it kills a lot of dealers. They sell their phones and services online cheaper than the price their independent dealers pay. Then the company expects these same dealers to provide free training for the online customers when they walk in with problems.

Somehow, the FCC looks past the way cell phone company mergers crush small, retail phone businesses. They permit near perfect monopolies that cause major channel conflict.

If you sell online for a set price, and you sell to your distributors for the same online price, there is no room left for their margin. To eliminate this conflict, you will need to set your online price high enough to make room for your wholesale distribution network to make money.

When you do have your first product that sells well on the Internet, you might get requests to buy your product in bulk for discounts. Be careful here, because you might find that those people will list your own product on eBay against you for less than your established retail price. If this happens, be sure to sit by the phone because your distributors will be calling soon. This is a form of channel conflict and you will lose money until the bulk-discount customers are out of inventory.

I have had this happen with one of my products. Someone bought one thousand parts with an agreement they would only sell them at retail stores, but the next day they had an eBay site selling them for two dollars less than my price. It is difficult to get that situation fixed via the eBay arbitration board – or at least I found that to be true.

⚑ #18 Shipping 🐵

If your product is less than thirteen ounces, I have found the US Post Office is the best way to ship, especially if you offer free shipping on eBay. Free shipping on eBay is a big deal because many sites charge more for shipping and handling than the cost of the product, and buyers watch for this.

I can ship a two ounce package anywhere in our fifty states for about $1.70 (which includes delivery confirmation), and PayPal allows me to print these labels directly from the US Post Office without having to re-enter the order details. I print labels every day while I am having my oatmeal. If your packages are more than thirteen ounces, then you can use regular parcel post services, also direct from the PayPal site or directly on sites like UPS and FedEx.

When it comes to shipping heavier packages, if you use someone like UPS, it is important to find out how they track your usage so you can qualify for shipping discounts. Just ask your local UPS rep. Don't expect training from your local, independently owned UPS store, because they do not make money if you do not use their store to package and ship.

Shipping offshore can be a nightmare. Again if it is a small package, I use the US Postal Service. They have a quick customs form that takes just a few seconds to fill out. I ship to countries all around the world. A typical three ounce shipment to India is about six dollars without delivery confirmation.

I want to offer free shipping everywhere, so I tell offshore customers, if they buy multiple parts, I will ship for free. I can afford to do this because with volume, I am making more money. Remember you are getting the distributors' and the retailers' share if you have set your pricing structure to avoid channel conflict.

⚑#19 Working With the Big Guys 👻

Selling to big box stores can be good news or a nightmare. Most of them do not treat you as an equal, or in some cases, even human. They have all the power unless you can establish a profitable, popular market on your own. After some level of success, you get some measure of pricing power when you go to see them or, when you are really successful, they might come to you.

Many of my big box customers seem to care only about price and ensuring that you are taking all the risk. Perhaps someday these giant retailers will understand the benefit of a more open door policy toward inventors, innovators, and entrepreneurs. I believe they would get more amazing products than they can imagine.

Also, many of them (or agents trying to sell to them on your behalf) will take your parts offshore in an attempt to get lower prices that do not include you. In some cases, the world of big retail does not include the concept of "loyalty" – which is why I tend to make big box stores my last option.

Having a patent will help but not necessarily stop big box stores from trying to bypass your rights and abuse your intellectual property. I like to keep something in the process as a trade secret, because even if they can get around your patent, if you keep how you are doing something in your process private, sooner or later, if they want to profit from the idea, they will need to work with you.

⚑ #20 Please Beam Me Someplace

Social media, blogging, Facebook, tweeting, and whatever is next are extremely important. But to be effective, it takes almost fulltime engagement. So, you can blog, tweet, work with existing distributors, sell to big box retailers, do cold calling, set up an Internet direct system or develop your own combination of several of these.

I suggest you get some help and write a social media master plan before you start. You need to make sure you plan to spend the time it takes to keep each one up to date. Any web site or social media tool not kept up to date is a real problem and you are probably better off not launching it in the first place.

⚑ #21 Being Paranoid about Sharing Your Idea 🙈🙈🙈

If you are trying to sell your idea to a large company, most will not sign a non-disclosure agreement. Some will welcome you if your patent has been issued but that can take years. I say don't worry so much about people stealing your idea because even if your invention is great, you are still going to have to convince them it is good for their bottom line. Keeping something in the process secret can also be a good thing to do.

I have used stop gap measures — like taking a detailed meeting agenda to the unveiling and asking an attendee to initial and date it. At least that shows when I was there and what we talked about. I know most lawyers will disagree with this tactic, but it is preferable to never showing your product.

Of course, working corporation to corporation is a different story and you need special, more elaborate precautions that involve the corporate legal staff.

⚑ #22 No Distribution Plan – Yikes! 🐵🐵🐵🐵

Distribution is critically important. Imagine having invented the light bulb or telephone at a time when there was no network of power or phone lines. Your first priority would be to make sure there is a plan to get wires to every home, factory and office so your invention can create market pull.

Your idea needs a functioning distribution network too. Without a distribution plan, even if your idea can grow hair on bald heads, it will not move off the shelf. So why not mock up the product and test distribution before you ransom your future?

I am in awe of distribution networks like that of Amway. I believe the day that Rich DeVos and Jay VanAndel developed a product in their garage, (so the story goes) they also invented one of the most efficient distribution systems the world has ever known. That one distribution concept has worked for thousands of products. Brilliant!

A few years ago, I had my first product on QVC and that was an eye-opening experience. Being on air was exciting, but the risk of saying the wrong thing was not the greatest risk.

Please remember, if you have the QVC opportunity, the financial risk is all yours. QVC will examine your product and tell you how many you are scheduled to sell. You have to manufacture that amount and put the finished product in their warehouse, all at your expense.

If you do not sell out or do not hit their "dollars per minute" sales threshold, all remaining stock is returned to you at your expense. I am not knocking QVC because that can be a great venue for distribution of product. I just want you to know that if you try

QVC, the risk is real – and should make you nervous, especially if you are a rookie.

There are many ways to distribute your products and services. However, the top five markets that you should consider include:

1. Direct to customers B2C
2. To other companies who sell to retail customers B2B2C
3. Direct to other businesses that use your product B2B
4. To wholesalers who sell to distributors
5. Unlimited combinations of all of the above

All have advantages and disadvantages. Just be sure to research and plan your distribution system as you do your product, and continually test the market so when you do spend money on a patent or expensive prototype, you will have a clear idea on the market.

The point is, distribution is just as important as your product idea. Don't take it lightly. And get some help if you need it, and trust me, you do.

It's as simple as this: distribution is the fuel that drives your new business world. I have stopped more ideas because of a distribution problem than for anything else. Here are two stories about the many things I have stopped because of distribution issues (it is not just about the idea).

Story Time

I stopped a Motorcycle Tie Down product that I still love

I have driven motorcycles most of my life and hauled them in trailers all over the country. By far, the most popular tie-down is a ratchet type that is hard to use because it jams the strap in the mechanism. Also, when you release the tension, it is a real finger pincher and it releases the load all at once, causing your motorcycle to jump to the opposite side and maybe even tip.

I have some experience in the boat winch business and created a miniature winch that works as a great tie-down. It uses seat belt harness material and works fantastic.

As I built prototypes and showed them to the distributors and retailers, they loved this new tie-down concept. However, based on my cost, by the time I sell to distributors who sell to retailers who sell it to end-users, the selling price goes up to twenty-five dollars.

Even though this was a better tie-down, by far, and distributors felt it could sell for a premium price, you can buy four of the old design tie-downs for twenty-five bucks. Even though it was a better idea, I decided not to move forward because I could not get distributors to take enough of the risk for this part.

If I had ignored distribution and focused only on the features, functions, and customer feedback, I would have spent a ton of money tooling and surely sold a few, but not enough to get the returns I needed to make it worthwhile. Meanwhile, I have the best motorcycle tie downs in the world and I am the only one using them.

Ratchet handle works in tight places

Holds twice as much with half the effort

Story Time

I stopped a Vehicle Garment Rod that many still love and use

If you make long trips, traveling by car, you know your back seat will be filled completely with hanging clothes. Existing garment rods retail for about ten dollars, but they fall down, bend, and do not work with all coat hooks and grab handles.

I designed a garment rod with an internal spring that presses out to lock on coat hooks or pulls in to lock on grab handles. It works with virtually all vehicles on the road today. It supports more weight than coat hooks are designed to hold, and will not fall down when you grab a handful of hangers while standing next to the car in a parking lot (while it is raining).

I built prototypes and gave them away to friends. Everyone that used them loved them and wanted more. But again, using a distribution system or even direct to retail, I could not get the cost low enough to be close to the $10 retail unit, even if we positioned it as a premium product at a higher price. So we did not move forward.

If I had listened to the people who were comparing features and benefits without the feedback from the distribution network, I could easily have spent serious money and THEN found out nobody would distribute my garment rods.

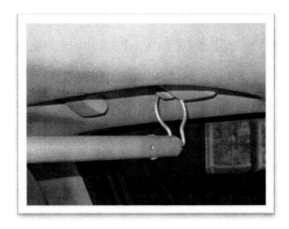

Presses out to lock on coat hooks

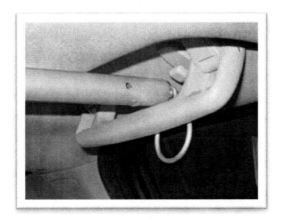

Pulls in to lock on grab handles

TIP: Even if your product is the "world's best," that might not be enough to make it in the market. Regardless of how well it is accepted during development, it is likely you are going to have to work harder to sell your product than you did to create the idea in the first place. If you do not want to market and sell your products personally, make sure you design your organization to include someone who really loves to sell.

Key Areas That will Enhance Success

Here are several important areas individuals and corporations can miss as they are doing due diligence on their ideas. Addressing these things up front can greatly enhance the success of the new venture you are considering. These areas do not comprise a magic formula and do not guarantee your results, but I promise, if you complete these steps, you will greatly increase your odds of success.

It All Begins With Quality Research

As inventors, we must consider that we might be powerless to be objective about the quality and practicality of our ideas because we are already convinced our ideas are winners. This is a real dilemma because we all need to have the confidence to believe in our dreams. Yet that same confidence can blind us to the reality of risk. If not careful, we will make decisions based on what we wish and pray will happen, instead of what is reasonable to expect. How can you deal with this?

If you are still a "go" after you do your own search, you might want to ask or hire someone to give you a second opinion.

In another life I used to trade spread options as a hobby (and still have most of my hair). Trading options can be a very complicated thing to do if you do not do it every day. To guard against doing something that would get us in trouble, we formed spread options teams so that someone else could check the trade we were about to make.

I suggest you consider using this team approach with the research you do. It is critical for you to find out if your idea was (or is) already in the market and if there are relevant existing patents. You may or may not be able to hire professionals to check your work, but having an "inventor buddy" can really help – and you can return the favor.

Research, when copied and added to your portfolio, will save you money and time as you go through this process. Patent attorneys will spend less time because of the research completed by you or someone you hired. Engineers will learn from what others have done. Suppliers will know what your competition is doing. The more research you do on your own, and the better your records, the less you will have to pay to other people to do that same work.

If you are still ready to move forward with your project, then find a patent search source and send your package to them to get your work verified. You can use a licensed patent agent or a patent attorney for your search. I have used both agents and attorneys for searches with success. To find one in your area, call local inventor groups or entrepreneurial start up associations, network with other inventors and interview a few. Patent agents are not permitted to do everything a licensed attorney can do, but some are just as good at searching and can cost less. Either way you go make sure to get a quote for the exact work you are asking them to do before you give them the go ahead.

Remember, the more work you do yourself, the better your agent's or attorney's results will be. If your idea is a physical product, you need to have an easy-to-understand sketch as well as a one page descriptor explaining the problem and solution. You'll find more on how to get that done later in this book.

A Few Thoughts About Patent Protection

Patents, when obtained, can be a deterrent to competitors and can be an asset for your company that you can sell with the idea. However, be careful when it comes to going to court to take infringement action. Some judges watch out for the little guy but my experience is that he with the biggest purse wins.

Good litigation attorneys can demand rates of several hundred dollars an hour (and like to work in packs). They expect huge, upfront retainer fees. Litigate if you must, but please don't trade everything you have to prove a point. You can go broke in the process – many do.

It is unlikely that, as an individual, you will have adequate funds to win a patent infringement suit against a corporate giant. It is just too expensive. I have been a witness for more patent infringement suits than I care to remember, and it is never fun.

Almost every patent infringement case, with which I have been involved, ends with a business agreement. The problem is that companies will spend millions on lawyers before they get to the business agreement point.

Many executives that manage patent infringement issues leave it up to their attorneys to figure out the business strategy. Guess what happens — long, drawn out litigation that takes years and, most of the time, adds questionable value in the end. Executives need to take charge of the strategy and use their attorneys as lawyers and not business strategy advisors – but that is just my opinion.

I am not suggesting your idea is not worth protecting. I am saying that individuals who go against corporations usually get crushed. It has been my experience that corporations that go against other corporations in patent litigation suits tend not to add in all the costs (like opportunities lost) when it comes to including the time, energy, and spirit it takes out of their companies.

It is hard to know when or when not to patent your idea. Because, most of the time you have to decide about whether to file for a patent early in the process and sometimes long before you have solid evidence that there is a market for our idea.

Corporations have more cash and most of the time have a much larger budget for patent filing and therefore tend to be a little quicker to file. Inventors who work alone with a much smaller budget have a bigger challenge. For the individual I recommend you find patent agents and patent attorneys that will interview you for free and have an understanding that getting a patent with no success in the market place has no value.

What does this mean when it comes to individuals getting a patent? Patents absolutely make a difference (especially utility patents). But, in my opinion, the biggest reason to patent is protection when there is evidence of a market. I realize market indicators can be hazy, but if there is no market you clearly do not need a patent.

Doing Consumer Market Testing

Doing consumer market testing is essential, even if you are going to sell your idea. If you test your idea with potential users and it does great, that is leverage you can use to ask more for your idea. Market testing makes forecasting future sales and profit much easier. You know the forecast has a high probability of being accurate when you can say you tested this with 200 potential users and got an 85% definite buy at $25.

Most corporations and large companies hire a marketing company to do focus group testing. A focus group is a small, cross section of people who fit your exact target market demographic.

Market research companies have the resources to find any demographic you need. You can sort by age, sex, income, family, education, and any other criteria. Focus group members are paid to sit in a conference room while a moderator shows them your product and leads a discussion about its merits and faults.

The product development team members sit outside the room, observing through a one-way glass. The glass, by the way, should be bulletproof, because I have watched some inventors lunge toward the glass when a participant trashes their idea.

In my opinion, focus groups work well when in the early stages of a design and you want directional input. The downsides are several: first it can be very expensive and second, an unskilled moderator might allow the participants to follow a controlling individual. Group members can quickly develop a herd mentality and go in an unexpected direction which is yet another reason to make sure you have a quality moderator to get things back in control.

If your product is ready to go and you want to test it, I suggest you consider a technique that will give you feedback from a larger sample of individuals. I have used mall-intercept product testing to great success for this purpose.

If you live near a shopping mall, call the office that manages the facility and ask if they permit product testing. Many say yes. If they do, ask them if they can suggest a marketing company that has done product testing in their facility before. This is a good place to start. I have used college marketing classes for this, and it works very well. Most professors are glad to help if they can, and their students get some firsthand experience interviewing consumers about a product. They also learn something about data collection and management.

You set up a booth with a sign that tells everyone what you are up to. On the sign, you indicate the type of person you need for your interview and the reward (if any) for participating. For example, if you are testing a toy for 10 - 12 year olds, your sign might say, *We will give you $5 for your 2 cents about our new toy if you have children with you between 10 and 12 years old.* You will be surprised how long people will stand in line for $5.

You don't always have to pay people to test products. It seems you can always find people at the mall, willing to talk to you about your project.

If you have never written a product survey questionnaire, I suggest you get some help. If you plan to use the results later to sell your idea, you must avoid leading questions or your market test could lose credibility.

Story Time

Doing Mall Intercept Product Testing

A few years back, I was a part of a group developing and launching a revolutionary electronic product. You probably use this product very day, but I did not obtain permission from the current owners to use the name so I will leave that unsaid.

This product required the users to interpret blinks of a light to determine when the product was ready to use. I wanted to test at least 200 users, so we went to a large, Midwest shopping mall and set up small, private booths to test six people simultaneously. Each booth had audio and video cameras monitored in a private screening room elsewhere in the mall. Here, engineers and designers could watch potential consumers try to use their design.

The testing process did its job very well but the product did not. People could not figure out the code of the blinking light. Most of them tried conscientiously, but failed after repeated attempts. In this case, private testing was effective. If you were to use a focus group to test a similar product, people confused by the blinking light might be embarrassed to say so in a group. That is why I prefer individual interviews when possible.

As I sat in the screening room watching the participants try to figure out this product, it was fascinating to watch the engineers react to the consumers' confusion.

If it had not been such an expensive, important project for our company, it would have been funny to watch these engineers and designers groan at the incompetence of these people that could not figure out how to use such a simple item. In fact, the lead electronic design engineer had to leave the mall due to frustration with watching "Those Incompetent People" test his product. In the end, he changed the user interface scheme and the product did very well in the follow up tests.

Some lessons learned using the mall intercept process:

1. When all was done, we showed excerpts from early (failed) tests and later (successful) tests to our customers. We proved our due diligence and received very high marks. The point is, even when tests reveal product shortcomings, they also show the best path to product improvement.

2. Sometimes, 12 people sitting around a table to test a product can unduly influence each other. When you do larger, quantitative tests, you can ask demographic questions at the start and slice your data to get the exact target market you need. This can be much less expensive than spending money to employ a marketing company to pre-sort candidates.

3. When exposing inventors to the process of market testing their own products, be sure to prep them to relax and take the experience as a data point and not a personal insult. It might be wise to keep anything that can be used as a weapon out of the screening room. I am not sure how beating a tester into liking your product would work, but I am sure mall security would have an opinion.

4. Write instructions and design user interface schemes to about an eighth-grade level. This is not a slam on the general public. It is just a fact that if you do this kind of testing you will get people that do not know their own address and phone numbers by heart. They are not bad or incompetent. They are your customers and you need them more than they need you.

5. *Design and test your product for every country, culture, income, educational level and age group in your target market.*

6. *If you test your product and the participants do not like it – don't blame them.*

Patent Searching for more than Patents

Go to *Google Patent Search* (it's free) and search using any criteria that relate to your idea. Save the first page and any drawings of relevant search results for each patent you find, because you will need this information when you build your patent comparison grid (see Figure 3 later). Key things to look for when searching include:

1. Issued Date – When this patent was issued and how much time is left on the life of the patent.

2. Determine who the Assignee is for this patent. Assignees can be an individual or a company.

3. Determine who the Inventor(s) are and:

- Call them and ask about the commercial success. If it did not sell, ask why they think it did not.

- Some of the individuals you call will hang up or tell you they cannot talk to you for legal reasons. That is okay. Just log your conversation in your journal and call the next name on the list. Eventually someone will talk.

4. Repeat this for every reference patent cited for this search. Just click on the highlighted patent number to go to the next patent.

There are two basic patent types - Utility patents (how something works) and Design patents (how something looks).

Utility patents are better for protection, can offer more value if you sell them, take more time, and cost more.

If you feel squeamish when I suggest you call strangers to ask about their patent and the success (or lack of it), you might not have the fortitude to keep going on your project.

I am not suggesting that you need to call other inventors to have your idea be a success. I am saying if "cold calling" people on the phone, in person, or at shows causes you concern you need to do one of the following:

1. Stop and go back to regularly scheduled life programming.
2. Partner with someone that loves doing the kinds of things you do not like to do.
3. Hire support when "cold calling" of any kind is necessary and, believe me, it will be.

When searching a utility patent, be sure to examine the claims section closely. That section usually reveals marketing strategy for the product.

Sample Design Patent:

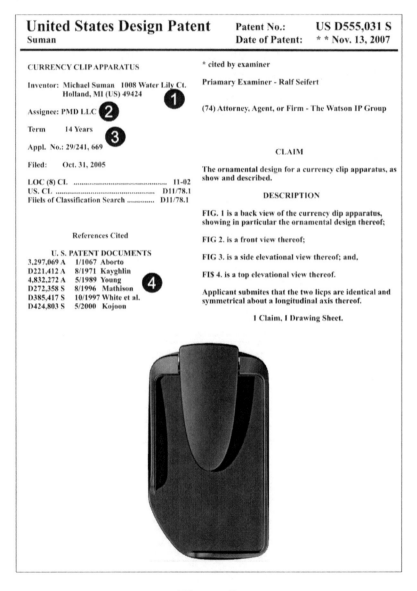

United States Design Patent
Suman

Patent No.: **US D555,031 S**
Date of Patent: * * Nov. 13, 2007

CURRENCY CLIP APPARATUS

Inventor: Michael Suman 1008 Water Lily Ct. Holland, MI (US) 49424

Assignee: PMD LLC

Term 14 Years

Appl. No.: 29/241, 669

Filed: Oct. 31, 2005

LOC (8) Cl. 11-02
US. CL D11/78.1
Fliels of Classification Search D11/78.1

References Cited

U. S. PATENT DOCUMENTS
3,297,069 A   1/1067   Aborto
D221,412 A   8/1971   Kayghlin
4,832,272 A   5/1989   Young
D272,358 S   8/1996   Mathison
D385,417 S   10/1997   White et al.
D424,803 S   5/2000   Kojoon

* cited by examiner

Priamary Examiner - Ralf Seifert

(74) Attorney, Agent, or Firm - The Watson IP Group

CLAIM

The ornamental design for a currency clip apparatus, as show and described.

DESCRIPTION

FIG. 1 is a back view of the currency dip apparatus, showing in particular the ornamental design thereof;

FIG 2. is a front view thereof;

FIG 3. is a side elevational view thereof; and,

FIS 4. is a top elevational view thereof.

Applicant submites that the two licps are identical and symmetrical about a longitudinal axis thereof.

1 Claim, I Drawing Sheet.

Figure 2

Using Business Search Tools

Use *ThomasNet* to find suppliers and customers. You can also use www.thomasnet.com as a tool to research competitors. It is also free.

You can sort by company name, function or drill down into more micro services by clicking on "related categories." *ThomasNet* provides a direct link to each company's web site.

This is a great tool for competitive analysis. For example, if you are developing a bathroom shower ring, you can enter that in the search field and go to dozens of web sites to see if anyone is already selling your idea.

Don't forget to print, copy, and log every site you go to as you will need it later (even if you do not find anything). It is also a great way to show due diligence to potential partners and investors.

Once you find the company's stock symbol from their web site (if they are public) you can use www.smartmoney.com to start your deep dive on any company, and yes it is free.

TIP: To grab full or partial images off your computer screen buy Snag It at www.techsmith.com. I realize some computers have screen grabbing features, but sometimes I just want a small piece of the page and this software works great.

Using Financial Sites as Business Research Tools

You can use sites like the www.smartmoney.com site to find details about the company you are going to call. You can find phone numbers, names of management, addresses, and how the company is doing financially. On the same site, you can read press releases that can contain all sorts of information you might need to know.

You can also use this site to learn more about someone who has a patent in your product market area, a potential supplier, or targeted customer.

If you look up a company on the *SmartMoney* site, and you want to expand your list of sales prospects, click on the COMPARE button and the site will automatically pick four competitors to the company you are researching. Plus, it will give you thirty financial comparisons to rank these companies. If you wonder what these financial metrics mean, just click on the name of the metric and a short definition will pop up.

Maybe you have targeted a potential customer because they already sell something similar to what you have developed and you think they might want a broader range of product. Or perhaps you want to sell to their competitor because the competitor wants a leg up on the leader. Either way, you can get much of the information you need here.

As with any of these tools, you might not get the answer to your specific questions, but by digging around you will be surprised what you find. Again, the *SmartMoney* site is only one possibility. There are dozens that do similar things.

Story Time

Research based Selling

I was hired by the President of an air compressor company to work with his sales people to help figure out what they might do to improve sales. During my interview with the President, he mentioned that two of his biggest frustrations were that he could not get any business from a huge global food processor located in his town, and that his salespeople were only selling on price.

I already had the sales seminar planned but I needed a strong closing statement that would get everyone thinking. The night before the presentation, I did a Google search by using the name of their targeted food processing company and the words "air compressor" in the search.

You guessed it. The first hit was a six-month old article in a financial newspaper talking about a blown seal in an air compressor. It sprayed oil over quite a bit of production, all of which had to be recalled at a cost of millions of dollars. I had my closing slide!

At the end of the training day I showed them the Google search but I told them that it was a fake. I said that I made it up to start a discussion. My question for them was two parts. First, if this article were true, would you still sell on low price? Second, how would you approach this customer if this article were true? The group immediately responded with comments like I would never sell on price if I knew they were having trouble with their existing supplier.

From there, they came up with many creative solutions. My favorite was that they stop selling air compressors and start selling clean, dry, compressed air with a guarantee against leaks. They were talking about moving from selling compressors and dryers to selling a service that requires no capital because their customers never own the equipment. Brilliant!

The excitement in the room was obvious. High fives were going around and everyone was ready to retire to the bar – but then the VP said "Guys – calm down remember Mike said this search was a fake" and the room went quiet.

I got everyone's attention as I was packing my projector and said, "As a summary, I have to tell all of you that I told you one lie today. My lie was that the article about your Holy Grail customer was not fake. It is true". I then handed out copies of the real report showing the oil leak problem. My last words as I walked out were, "So what are you going to do about it?" The room was again filled with a hopeful positive attitude, they could not wait to get at that customer and selling low price was no longer an issue!

My point is, they had been selling air compressors based on capital cost, warranty, and performance, but they ended up solving a huge pain point and selling a service.

All of this was made possible with a simple information search that took five seconds and was free.

Creating a Competitive Matrix

Patent Market Comparison Matrix								
Patent Number	Inventor	Name and Brand	Assignee	Date Issued	Years Left	Is it in the Market	How our product differs
DXXX,XXX	Bob Smith	Snapper Mixer	Crunch Corp	Sep-80	None	No	More colors
XXX,XXX	Dick Brown	MixMaster	Watson Foods	Nov-92	None	No	Faster and more speeds
XXX,XXX	Charlie Chan	Master Mixer	Food Flingers	Dec-03	15	Yes	Less expensive

Figure 3

By now you should have enough information to create a competitive matrix like the one shown in Figure 3. This is a great way to show that you have done your due diligence on the product side but also information on the existing players. This is also a good tool to put in your business plan. Obviously the sample in Figure 3 is fake, but it is easy to make up your own.

If you cannot find this kind of information about the market you have in mind, I suggest you consider putting your project on hold until you do. Why would you invest in your product when you have no idea who is out there and what the market is currently doing? But let's assume you have your competitive matrix and now you can keep moving forward.

Now that you have that done, keep moving by:

1. Looking in all the retail and online stores you can find

2. Buying all industry magazines that apply

3. Buying all the competitive products you can find

4. Attending industry trade shows and while at the show make sure you:

- Search for potential distributors using your fake advertisement (more on this later). When showing your problem / solution visual, keep how you are solving the solution a secret. Example: The problem is darkness, your solution is your light bulb, but do not disclose how you are extruding the tungsten filament as that might start your "sale date" for your patent clock (which is one year after you offer it for sale).

- In the booth, ask attendees if they think there is a market at your retail price. Bring home a stack of distributors cards for follow up when the time is right. If nobody shows interest, you are getting a clear signal that there might be a problem.

More on attending Industry Trade Shows

Be sure to attend industry trade shows that fit your target market. It is easy and relatively cheap. If you live in the Midwest, industry trade shows are held in Chicago, Detroit, Cleveland, Indianapolis, and every other city with a convention center — all of them easy to reach with a tank or two of gas.

As an example, if you live in the Midwest and Chicago makes sense, go to www.mccormickplace.com and click on the calendar tab. Then click on the Year tab and all the events will pop up for that year. From there you can go to the organization that is sponsoring the show you want to see. Fill in a request for a pass to attend the show only. With many shows, the pass is free if the request is early.

Even though there may be some cost, industry trade shows are still the cheapest way to learn vital details about the industry you want to enter. The shows will reveal competitive products, potential suppliers or partners, but most importantly, they give you the opportunity to look for distributors.

I find it hard to believe that very few of the companies I have worked with allow or encourage their R&D people to attend industry trade shows.

If you do not want to take the time and effort to go to your industry trade show – you are asking to be surprised later in a way that might make you wish you would have never started this venture. Jot down all the reasons you do not want to go to your industry trade show before you start spending real money, then take the list and throw it away and go anyway.

Prototype Your Marketing Message Early

Even before your idea is ready to sell, you need to take your vision to distributors, investors, and everyone else you can corner to get help. It is important to show your idea with a clear and exciting message when you start making these contacts. A great way to accomplish this is to create a test advertisement. Here are some suggestions to help you get started:

Hire a marketing illustrator or advertising professional to help create this test (fake because it is early) advertisement. Find someone you can rent for one day. Have all your information in an easy-to-understand format. Just sketch what you think the advertisement should look like. Don't worry about your drawing ability. Your professional will take it to the next level.

Give them all the competitive, patent, and research information you have acquired. The more you give them the faster, cheaper, and more powerful your final result will be. I have employed college students to do this for very little money. Components of these early advertisements are the same as we learned in advertising 101:

1. You need to grab attention.

2. You need to show the problem and exhibit your solution.

3. Incorporate a "Surprise and Delight" feeling, with the help of your advertising support person.

4. Readers must "get it" in five seconds or less (as if flipping through a magazine).

5. This message should include a "Call to Action" (What do you want the reader to do?)

6. What can you say that your competitors cannot say?

Don't spend a lot of money on this step. Look for a marketing-advertising company that will work with you on prototype basis instead of a retainer contract relationship. And do it in one day!

You can use this fake advertisement in all areas of your new business development process for example:

- Getting your team focused on common value mission. I have posted test advertisements in cafeterias and gone back to my office, waiting for the upset people to come and tell me "this is not what we are thinking!" A test ad is a great tool to get more critiques at the critical, earlier stages of development. When people see an idea in the form of a four color advertisement, they are conditioned to think the product is in the market and react accordingly, without challenging the status – try it!

- Survey distributors at shows. Be careful to not leave copies of your early advertisement at the show or you might give a competitor some good ideas.

- Get suppliers interested and focused on your goals. When you show them your advertisement, they get what you are doing and it can really help.

- Pitch your value story to investors. Some investors are interested in verified facts only. When you have an advertisement on the cover of the executive section of your term sheet, it can provide a new and exciting perspective.

- Building a team can be a lot easier when positive buzz about your new business starts bubbling up. Your test advertisement can really help here.

- A test ad is a highly effective presentation tool to start the selling process. Think of your fake ad as a great visual elevator speech.

- When you leave your customer's office, after your presentation, the people in the meeting room where you presented are now your inside salespeople. An early advertisement can be an exciting tool for your customer to use to pitch to their bosses!

- Polish your value story. As you use this test advertisement throughout the product and business development phases of your project, the message will continually evolve. That is a great thing because, at the end, when you are ready to go to market and start PR, you have already created a great history of visuals and value storytelling.

Story Time

Prototyping a Test Advertisement

I was in charge of selling advanced products for a multi-billion dollar company. I had an idea that I pitched to the President of a division that was in a different market. I got along great with this guy, but he had no interest in starting a new product. The idea was to blend one of the products from our division with one of his products. He was simply not interested.

I had our marketing group design a test advertisement showing this product and attach it in a real industry magazine with the corporate logo of his biggest competitor.

The next time we had a lunch I casually pulled out the magazine and reminded him of the time I wanted to do this product with him — but as you can see your biggest competitor beat us to it.

What followed was more than I planned on. He got up and ranted and yelled about how he should have listened to me. He really pitched a fit to the point where I did not want to tell him it was a fake — but I had to.

So I told him it was a mock up and we shared a nervous laugh (whew). At that same lunch we put together a plan to launch the new product. It was picked up as an exclusive with a national distributor and ran for years.

TIP: *Do not underestimate the power of an advertisement that looks real and has the right marketing components. In this case the product was sold with no business case and no prototype — just a four color vision with a profit plan we scratched out on a napkin during that same lunch.*

A Better Way to Sell At Home and Away

What I mean by selling at home and away is if you are working alone or for a company you will need to sell inside (home) your own company to get the approvals and support you need. When you are ready to go to market you will be selling in the market (away).

There are literally thousands of books written on selling. I teach seminars on selling value, a process that would be impossible to explain in a few pages, but let me give you the key points.

Sell to Eliminate Customer Pain Points

Effective selling requires an investment of time before the sales call, researching the company and individuals to whom you are selling. You need to find out everything you can, but especially their "pain points." You can use the web sites mentioned in this book to find some pain points.

For example, using the *SmartMoney* site you might discover the company is capital-strapped. So, perhaps you want to be ready to amortize their investment. Or, you find on a Google search that the company lost some business because of a quality problem. So, you might want to include an extended warranty with product validation from a third-party test lab.

There are many potential methods of finding pain points. Interviewing for pain points takes some practice, but you can master this method quickly. Ask open- ended questions and then listen. The potential customer will get around to telling you what you need to hear. The "L" in a business lunch stands for LISTEN.

STOP Feature/Benefit Selling

You must consider stopping feature/benefit selling. Feature/benefit selling does not secure a long term customer relationship or position you as a problem-solver.

Feature/ Benefit selling is very risky, even if you think you know exactly what your competitors are selling and everything they are developing for the future. Remember, your customers almost always know more about your competitors than you do – even if that is not true you must behave as if it is!

After several selling visits, you might hear your customers say something like *there is nothing new* with your product plus *they have seen the same thing from others, only cheaper.* It is much harder for them to say this if you are focused on *their* pain points rather than *your* product's features and benefits. Customer-centric strategies win.

When you sell on low price based on features and benefits you can get caught in the famous "price reduction loop". It works like this; just when you think you are out of the running, you get a call telling you that you made the "Short List" which is code for more price negotiations. When selling based on price you have no idea if you are in the running or not. Your pricing might be used as a lever to get your competitors prices lower. Some fun!

Time is on your customer's side. Price beatings continue and you wonder if it is all worth it. In the end, you give away most of your margin, and you justify this by telling yourself at least you are still in the game.

Just when you are ready to give up again, you find out you made the "Yours to Lose" list resulting in more cost reduction rounds.

When you get the order you might not have any idea if it is good news or bad news – and neither does your boss but your CFO has an opinion and is looking for you to share it.

Are we having fun yet?

Consider Selling Using Prescriptive Relationships

Prescriptive Relationship selling is about solving customer problems as a consultant. You are shining a spotlight on their problem, not on your product (until the time is right). You are on their team, not an outsider trying to make a commission on a product. When you prove you understand the customer pain points and have a realistic prescription, you've made the sale without reducing the value of your solution.

Do your homework (searching for pain points) and then:

Deliver the post exam consultation using a corporate x-ray to deliver the prognosis and show the pain points you uncovered. If your doctor told you he found something on your x-ray and he would like you to see a specialist, you would jump at the recommendation.

Your calendar and checkbook would be wide open. You would be ready to do anything. He found your potential problems. You believed him and are ready to do whatever you need to do. That is selling based on a plan to remove your personal pain points and not the features or price of treatment he is going to recommend.

Imagine having a "features/benefits doctor." When he walks into the room, and before he examines you, he starts selling you a drug by telling you what is in it, how much it costs, and why he is qualified to deliver it to you. You would be confused and wonder if he was moonlighting as a representative for a drug company. Yet that is exactly how you sound when you sell using features and benefits of your product before you examine the patient and look for pain points. Only then can you discuss how your product is going to be the right prescription to alleviate the pain for your customer.

You perform the role of the specialist delivering your expert analysis of what must be done to relive the pain. Of course, your prescription is code for your products or services.

You keep the x-ray around that shows the root cause of the pain because you will need it later as low pricing battles creep back in the process. Left unchecked your customer will always revert to buying a product based on her interpretation of value – not yours.

That last statement is so important I am going to repeat it in **BOLD**.

Left unchecked your customer will always revert to buying a product based on her interpretation of value – not yours.

After you get the order, you schedule monthly follow up checks to look for early symptoms of pain reoccurrences so you can adjust your prescription.

That's it! Don't make selling more complicated than solving someone's problem. Prescriptive selling can be more than work than feature/benefit selling, but much more effective.

Story Time

Prescriptive Selling

We were selling a floor console that fit between the front seats of a compact model car to an automotive company. During the launch meeting we discovered that the four-wheel drive selector was to be a new kind of device. For the first time, it would be an electric switch. However, the customer believed the floor console was not the best place for this new switch. The meeting came to a standstill and our floor console business was in jeopardy.

It just happened that we supplied the overhead (between the visors) map lamp display. We needed to take the focus away from stopping the project. So, in the meeting, I made an announcement that there is a good chance we could locate the switch in our overhead map lamp display. To remove an obvious pain point that I anticipated, I went on to say that we would take care of the communication link to the shifter logic box that would be mounted in our floor console. I proposed to have a non-working prototype in one week, complete with a strategy to sell all the other relevant groups, inside our customer's company.

With some miracles and all-nighters by our designers, engineers and model builders, we had a great story ready for the next meeting. We kept the overhead display business, incorporated the switch, got the floor console business and it lasted for seven years. Plus, we positioned ourselves as the "go to" group to design and install electronic four wheel drive shift systems.

This was selling by problem solving. We did not talk about how the switch would work and be backlit for night use, color or shape of the button, or tooling, or piece cost. Cost was not on the x-ray. This was about integrating a selector switch without tearing up anything else in the vehicle designed by this team.

Part of our pain removal process was to ensure that we could negotiate deals within their company, even when their internal political issues usually prevented things from getting done. Using feature benefit selling we would have not discussed how we could get system approvals inside their company better than they could.

This is a great example of taking an x-ray of a customer, seeing their pain points, and developing a prescription that solves the problem. The old way of selling by features might have had us trying to convince our customer that it was okay to put an electric switch in our floor console down by the driver's knees and how cheaply we could do that – which, thankfully, is exactly what our competitors tried to do.

Pain Point Identification

If you are in a corporate structure, ask your own people to tell you their pain points. In other words, just ask the leaders of the divisions in your own company what keeps them up at night. I have never met a buyer who loses sleep over paying a few cents more for something. But the good ones do stay awake about bad or late material shutting down their operation.

Even if you are selling to a large retailer, you can find pain points. For example, some retailers you want to work with are not totally about price. They book profit from the sale of your product and put that profit into their plan. If you miss a delivery date or ship poor quality and they miss their targeted profit plan – it generates a pain point for them and you.

Identifying customer pain points is different for each industry, division and group. Start with how each group gets measured.

The following list shows examples of measurements for various groups you will encounter. With this list in mind, you may find that the customer's Purchasing group is struggling with one of your competitors because of slow delivery. You could use that in your pitch. Or if their Sales group is struggling with slow sales growth, you might do some market testing that shows how they can use your product to expand their sales.

Here are a few examples of how to search for potential pain points by considering how each group is measured. If any of these groups fail to perform to expected measurements, it creates a pain point for them:

Purchasing gets measured on cost, delivery, quality, continuous improvement, and terms.

Engineering gets measured on CAD accuracy, fit and function, reliability, change management, and bill of material costs.

Manufacturing gets measured on quality, delivery, inventory turns, and throughput.

Design gets measured on fit and finish, customer acceptance, theme accuracy, and Surprise and Delight.

Management gets measured on profit, market share, growth, efficiency improvement, cash flow, and culture.

Sales gets measured on identifying opportunities, sales growth, low customer churn, and receivables status.

Finance gets measured on accuracy of business case, profit contribution, and being the voice of financial reality even if the message might not be pretty at times.

When you really understand your customer's pain points, the need to sell ceases, because you truly know what your customers need. Instead of selling what you need to sell so you can make your goals, you deliver what your customers need to make theirs. And I promise they will love you for it.

The point here is: When your customer's pain points drive your product innovation the need to sell goes away!

This last line is so important I am going to repeat it in bold.

When your customers' pain points drive your product innovation, the need to sell goes away!

The Customer Value Decision Matrix

Develop your Customer's Value Decision Matrix before they do and keep yours private. Be sure to include the specific pain points on which you can improve. If you have done the research, your customers will recognize the painful truth of their problems in your presentation. Your matrix may reflect their internal documents — always a surprise to customers — or may expose emerging problems they have not considered — a reason to be grateful to you.

What you need to know to build your matrix and why you need one:

1. Do you know how your customers are going to measure you against your competitors? This is a "must know" so you can emphasize your good differentiators and improve the areas you do not measure up.

2. Ask your sales group why you lost recent orders and add those issues to the matrix. Your sales group will know why you lost business to this customer in the past. When you lose business it can be very painful, but it is also a perfect time to find out why so you can fix the issues if it makes sense to do so.

3. How can you identify the competition? Ask your customers who else is quoting and then start with www.thomasnet.net to find companies. Of course some customers will not share their decision matrix metrics (other than price, of course). But regardless of how you find them, go to www.smartmoney.com to research them.

4. Rank yourself against each competitor for each Value Metric.

5. Develop your prescriptive selling strategy based on how your differentiators will remove your customer's pain points better than anyone else can.

You can start your Customer Value Decision Matrix with the pain points in the chart showing in Figure 4, but they will be different for every company, industry and product. You must create your own pain points that are specific to your customers. Again, just ask open questions and listen. I have even asked customers for a sample of their decision matrix grid and, occasionally, they've given me a copy. Even if your customers are not using this type of matrix formally, they are doing it in some other form. You must find out how they rank you **before** they make sourcing decisions — so you can adjust.

If you work alone, and this ranking shows you in the least likely position to get the business, you should STOP and evaluate your value offering.

If you work in a corporation, and your company comes up last in your matrix, you need to get someone's attention fast. I know this is going to sound strange, but it is not unusual for a company to ignore signals that show them at a disadvantage. They dismiss it as bad information or bias.

If you are low on the matrix, do whatever you must to get this message across to management. Buy a copy of this book, highlight this area and leave it at your manager's door. Just kidding, (sort of) but you cannot let this pass because a poor ranking on a competitive matrix is an early indicator of major future problems. Without quick action, it will only get worse!

Your Customer's Value Decision Matrix					
	Value Metric (Pain Points)	Supplier Forced Ranking (1 is Best)			
		You	A	B	C
1	Percent Market Share	3	1	2	4
2	Responsiveness	1	2	3	4
3	Inventory Turn Mgmt	3	4	2	1
4	Tooling Capability	4	3	1	2
5	Global Supply Capability	4	1	3	2
6	Engineering Capability	4	3	2	1
7	Patent Hostage Potential	2	3	4	1
8	Quality	4	2	1	3
9	On Time Delivery	1	3	2	4
10	Marketing Support	2	1	4	3
11	Financial Soundness	3	2	1	4
12	Trust	4	3	2	1
	Grid Leader	35	28	27	30

Figure 4

Story Time

Using Pain Points to Sell

When I was starting to develop the idea of prescriptive selling based on pain points, I owned a small motor home. I did not like any of the stabilizing jacks I could find or afford.

I designed what I thought was a pretty nice product and made some prototypes. I used the levelers for a season and almost everyone I met while traveling that summer wanted a set. I made some improvements and got it ready to market. Conventional thinking would say I should produce some marketing materials, make some appointments and start making sales calls. But I thought I would try something different so ...

I made an appointment with the owner of the company that made what I thought was the worst leveler jack in the market. When I met with him the first time, I did not take my parts to the meeting because I did not know enough about his company's pain points to create a prescription for him.

During the meeting I told him I was an RV owner and had never found a leveler that I liked. If I found one, it was too expensive. During our conversation I found that the company owner had a real desire to have a "best in class" product and was willing to talk to me about a license.

We agreed to meet the next Saturday, which meant I had a lot of work to do. His pain points were several, but mostly he wanted a product that he could make using his existing manufacturing processes. He wanted to lift more weight with less effort by the user. And finally, he wanted to have a "surprise and delight" display to use at an upcoming trade show.

I had the "best in class" pain point solved because my design could lift 50% more than his product with much less cranking effort. Also, my design would already work perfectly with his existing manufacturing process. All I needed was a good display that would allow him to show this great new design to his customers at the upcoming show.

Working fast I fabricated a nice looking metal frame with a digital pressure readout display. When I went back for the next meeting I asked him to put his product in the frame. With the pressure readout display turned off I asked him to crank it until he would guess it was lifting 1000 pounds. He cranked it as hard as he could and when I turned on the display, it said 900 pounds and he was pretty pleased.

I then replaced his product with my design and turned off the display. I asked him to crank it until he guessed it would read 1000 pounds. He cranked it pretty hard and when I turned on the display and it read 1600 pounds. He was sold.

During the next few hours we wrote up an agreement on the spot and I walked out that same day with a check for $25,000 and 5% of sales for the next five years.

The point of this story is, I sold this product by creating it, fitting it to his manufacturing process, developing a market presentation tool and a selling strategy for his customers. In other words I was focusing on how I could help his company be successful instead of focusing on what I needed to win. In the end we both won.

Conventional selling would have had me showing off my sample during the first meeting. I would have talked about how great it was using feature / benefit selling. I would have missed his need to stay within his existing manufacturing process, his need to get something to the trade show quickly, and a way to display the differentiators. The challenge in this case was that my jack cost twice as much as his and if I would have started with features and price I would not have gotten past first base.

I also added a surprise and delight feature for his customers. I came up with an off-the-shelf, blow molded storage case, a branded cleaning rag and a small tube of lubricant for cleaning and maintenance.

In summary, instead of selling the functions of my leveling system, I offered these prescriptive solutions based on his pain points:

1. *Evidence of competitive metrics and differentiators in his favor*

2. *Claims that used independent testing*

3. *Great new tools to enhance his brand name*

4. *A product that fit his existing manufacturing process*

5. *An exciting point of purchase display*

6. *A storage case for customer use*

7. *A cleaning cloth lubricant as a purchase incentive for his customers*

Selling after your examination for pain points makes more sense than selling based on features and benefits – it just does!

Positioning yourself as a consultant — looking for solutions instead of a sales person looking for a commission — can form a relationship that lasts.

Sell With Evidence, Not Just Hype

Many inventors I meet tend to oversell the value story of what their new product or service can do. When you get a new idea for a product, you are the only person in the universe with that thought.

From the start, your challenge is to begin convincing the rest of the world, one person at a time, there is merit to your idea. Not only can that be a huge task, but it can feel like a very lonely place, because there are no facts yet.

In the beginning, it is just a vision. If you do not build evidence around this idea, people will start to question the validity of the idea as soon as you share the vision. Without solid evidence, you can become guilty of overselling — which in the end can make it easy for others to dismiss you as a great idea person but without real business acumen.

An example of overselling is to provide specific answers to questions when it is obvious there are no facts to back up the answers. I have watched this happen in the boardroom. After the meeting, someone needs to tell the presenter that nobody believed her. It is sad to watch an innovator who gets an opportunity to finally present to the executives, lose credibility and leave thinking it went well.

The solution to overselling is easy. First of all, just be aware that we all are guilty of overselling. You can also show a list of assumptions on which you base your comments. You might say there is a fifty-fifty chance that oil prices are going to double next year. Based on that assumption, your business case would be accurate. Of course, people will challenge your assumptions by requesting you rerun the numbers assuming a 25% oil increase. But at least they will know you are a capable business developer with a program that has perhaps has some flawed assumptions.

Let Them Tell You What They Want To Hear   You are not likely to sell your solution at the first pitch. Tell a compelling value story using the visual tools and prototype aimed at prescriptive pain removal. Then ask what they think. If they are not sold, ask why! At that point, listen very closely to what they are really telling you, because it is exactly what you need to change to get the sale. Now just go do it.

Tailor Your Pitch To The Group   Spend some time understanding your target audience and their pain points. Everyone you talk to wants to hear something that applies to them specifically. Take a minute to think how your "elevator pitch" needs to be changed, based on the group you are addressing.

For example, if you were selling a cup holder to an automotive engineering customer, you would talk about the fact that your design can hold a six ounce coffee cup and up to a sixty-four ounce Slurpee. On the flip side you would not ask engineering for an annual volume commitment because that is not what they do.

The point is, you should tailor your pain removal service to the pain points of each group. Pain point generalization is ineffective across groups.

Story Time

Selling with Evidence

I was in charge of sales to one of the top vehicle manufacturers in the world. We had our monthly general session that included a luxury assembly plant manager letting all the suppliers have it with both barrels.

He was berating all the suppliers in the audience. His plant was filled with inventory, much of which included bad parts and wrong colors. They were out of space on the assembly line staging points, and, of course, costs were out of line. It was a speech we had all heard before.

He had a fiery personality and most people stayed clear of him. I knew him slightly, and thought he respected our company. During this particular session I was starting to get concerned about his health because the more excited he got the higher his voice went up to the point that only dogs and superman could hear him.

After the session, I broke ranks and followed him to his office. I asked him if he was OK. He seemed a little surprised, but gave me (the Cliffs Notes) version of the same speech, but this time I could probe for pain points and found plenty.

I asked him if we came up with a method of removing a couple of hundred part numbers from his plant and freeing up one or two car links on the final assembly line, would he take time to listen. His exact response was, "Son, if you could do that, I would lick a spark plug. I sure as hell would meet with you but do NOT waste my time."

We already supplied all the components in the overhead interior of the vehicles in this plant — visors, map lamps, grab handles, coat hooks, and overhead displays for compass and outside temperature readouts.

Back at home, our team got together and created a solution that involved pre-mounting all of the overhead components on an empty headliner. We would include all wiring for the overhead computer displays and all lighting components. Then, we could ship them as one part called an Overhead System with only one part number for each color which would remove hundreds of part numbers from this plant.

As it turned out, we could eliminate almost five-hundred part numbers. We also saved four vehicle spaces on the final assembly line by removing the space needed for small part staging. The solution saved piece cost, reduced labor, and increased quality for the manufacturer.

We not only got the Overhead Systems business for this plant, our sub-assembly technique spread quickly to many other car manufacturers and is being used today on a global basis.

The point is, everyone else heard him at the meeting ranting about quality, too many parts being shipped to the plant, and no space. Our competitors went back to their companies and said they needed to use smaller boxes, fewer parts in staging, better quality, and of course, lower price.

I heard "don't fix the existing problem by increasing efficiency of a bad process – change the game." He held up his x-ray of his plant, and we developed a prescription while everyone else tried their best to improve efficiency of a bad system. In the end we both got leaner, more efficient, more flexible, and improved quality. Both our company and our customer became more profitable.

Partners and Contracts

Developing partnerships, joint ventures, and supply contracts can produce a lot of emotion and feelings of "we invented this, now we are giving it away." Because of all the emotion these deals can invoke, it is important to establish a step-by-step process that could be managed by a third party if needed.

It is also important to use a well-defined value identification process so the participants do not feel like this is a "who yells the loudest" negotiation.

The goal is to use a transparent, fully defined process. All parties must agree to value contribution points, weight them, and determine how long each value contribution point should get rewarded. Use the steps below to fill out your own partnering matrix shown in Fig 5:

1. Determine value areas by listing each value contribution point. Once this process is started, the tension usually leaves the room. There will still be disagreements but they will be about micro issues regarding value contribution ratios. However the emotional macro "we deserve most of the value" arguments are much less intense.

2. Determine the life of the program. Ten years was used on the example in Fig 5.

3. Determine the *investment split* and *percentage contribution* for each company involved for each value point.

4. Determine *payback time* for each *value contribution*. For example, engineering might stop spending money in one year but sales costs go on as long as the program runs.

5. Calculate the *payback split* based on *market life participation* for each *investment value* area. For example, if this is a ten-year program and the first value change is after two years in the market, then anything after the first two years would be pro-rated based on the contributions of the last eight years of value.

6. Do the math and calculate *share change* over time based on *value contribution end points* and calculated share changes at each of those points.

7. Give this to your attorney and you will save a lot of money. You will also get a preliminary contract based on agreed upon starting shares and how those shares change over time. You will get this without most of the emotion and legal wrangling that can accompany a non-structured agreement development process.

I have seen many businesses struggle because they did not do this in the beginning. If you try to get this done in the beginning and don't get it done – you will be doing it later, just with many more lawyers involved.

TIP: Both sides drawing up agreement proposals and letting attorneys volley for months is not the most efficient process – but widely used. Why not get both companies' decision makers in the room and use a non threatening process managed by a neutral party and give the results to the legal group with a mandate to make it work?

Balancing Partnering Contribution Value			
Value Area	Company A	Company B	Pay Back Time Frame (years)
The Idea	100%	0%	10
Business Case Development	50%	50%	2
Design and Engineering	100%	0%	2
Tooling	100%	0%	4
Manufacturing	0%	100%	10
Distribution	0%	100%	10
Warranty	0%	100%	10
Sales	0%	100%	10
Marketing	50%	50%	4
Cash	50%	50%	10
	45%	55%	
Percent of Market Life			No of splits
20%	45%	55%	10
40%	37.5%	62.5%	8
60%	25%	75%	6
80%	25%	75%	6
100%	24%	76%	6

Figure 5

Story Time

Partnering Balance

Some brilliant engineers on my product development team invented a great electronic product. This product was going to be a fantastic "add in" to the parts we already sold inside vehicles. We also knew that for us to get penetration across the entire industry, the car companies would insist that we license the product to other suppliers to incorporate our idea into their parts.

As you can imagine, the prospect of revealing our intellectual property made everyone feel territorial and defensive. The general sentiment from my company was "We spent the time and money inventing this once-in-a-lifetime product and the client wants us to give it away. Our competitors are just going to steal it from us!"

There is nothing harder than being forced to license a new technology to your most talented competitors. I was in charge of putting these license deals together with companies that, to say the least, did not like the idea of working together. It is a lot like being a dating service for people who were once married to each other.

The problem was complicated, but we had to start somewhere. Listing the value contribution areas was a good start. With the decision makers in the room, we started by listing the value components. For example:

- *Who invented the part?*
- *Who is going to engineer this package?*
- *Who is going to pay for the tooling for this application?*
- *Who is going to market this licensed part?*

Soon, everyone in the room was suggesting areas of value contribution. Some suggestions went on the list quickly. Some were debated, then added, and some were thrown out. But we were gaining ground because we all were using the same process.

Then we decided on how long each value area should be paid. Eventually the mood in the room went from mistrust and concern to team problem solving. At the end of the afternoon, we just did the math and everyone took a copy home. After some changes, we had everything we needed to give to the lawyers to draw up a license agreement.

As an example let's say we agreed to sell the part to them for $10 and they would sell it for $28. The $18 gross profit was split 45/55 the first two years, and 37.5/67.5 from years 3 and 4 and so on.

TIP: *When you license a competitor, you eliminate potential patent infringement from that company because, during the license agreement process, you include a non-compete clause.*

Break Time – We Are Half Way

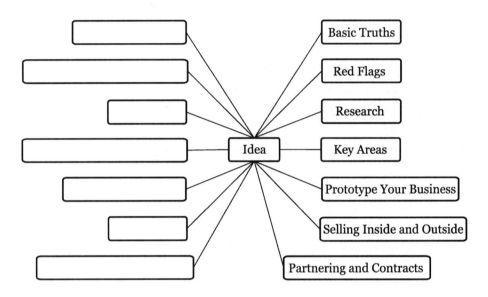

Congratulations we are half way through the chart. I hope you picked up some pointers so far.

Build It Quick and Fail Even Faster

Do NOT spend a great deal of time and money on early prototypes because you are going to build several versions. Also, you need to prototype every component of your business – not just the product.

Here are some thoughts about turning your idea into a 3-D mockup and getting to the testing phase quickly.

- The early models do not have to be beautiful or totally functional.

- Spend as little as possible on first samples. There will be many more to come.

- Look for self-employed designers, engineers, and model builders. Be sure to tell them exactly what you want and get "not to exceed" quotes.

- Test your prototype formally or informally. The best way to do this is with distribution channels. Be careful testing your idea with people that love you – some tend to be less than honest. Celebrate that someone loves you though!

- Don't give up if your early prototypes get bad reviews. These are teaching moments.

- Don't stiff arm the devil's advocates that show up – they might be right! If they are right, that does not necessarily mean stop. It might mean reset your navigation system. As a test, when this happens, write down what your devil's advocate does not like about your project. Then write your side of the story, explaining why you disagree with those issues. Then find an independent third party to read both sides and give you an opinion about which side is more reasonable. Again, as an inventor, you are vulnerable when it comes to believing your own press. Find someone who has no dog in the fight.

TIP: Try not to waste your energy pushing back against people that disagree with you. Be aware that they might be right. But, more importantly, if you redirect their energy by asking them to help, the results can be amazing. Leave your ego in the parking lot! This is a lesson I learned later in life that I wish I would have understood much earlier.

Story Time

Prototype in One Day

Making a prototype does not necessarily take weeks, or even several days. Here is how a product development company created a one-day process. They started with a request to build a prototype of a hand-held diesel engine analyzer to get market feedback quickly, while spending the least amount of money possible.

The manager called two software engineers, a mechanical engineer, and an industrial designer to his desk at eight in the morning. He asked the designer and engineer to be back at his desk at noon with the best mockup possible. He gave them the specifications and they were off.

He gave the two software engineers a stack of three-by-five cards, a functional specification, and wrote (off/on) on the first card. He asked them to use the cards to create a tree diagram to simulate the user interface scheme.

At noon, they were all back. The designer and engineer had a mock up made with cardboard, tape, a fake cord, they did things like place lead inside their box to simulate the projected weight. They did an amazing job with the time and funding they had.

The software engineers made their functional tree diagram as best they could in the time allowed. It should be noted that all four team members had fun but were very skeptical of the value of their mock ups.

At noon, they all got in a company van (with some box lunches to save even more time) and drove to three diesel engine repair shops. *They offered the manager money to rent one of their mechanics for thirty minutes for an interview about the value of the proposed analyzer unit.*

All three shops provided a mechanic and the manager at no charge and spent thirty minutes (and no more) providing feedback.

At the end of the day, they had spent forty dollars on materials and received three great pieces of market feedback. Just a few years ago, it would have cost $100,000 and probably taken at least 6 months to do the same research. Looking back on that day, it seemed that all involved knew the old way of developing products had changed forever.

Prototype Your Business Not Just the Part

Find suppliers (designers, engineers, marketers) willing to add the one-day prototype process to their service story. Prepare a prototype package for all phases of your business. In each package, include all of the work you have done to date, with a clear explanation of what you are asking from each supplier. If you don't specify exactly what you want, the costs will skyrocket. For example, if you go to a photographer without exact details of the shots you want, they will spend a lot of time asking you what you want. The more time they spend trying to find out what you want, the more money they will need to charge you.

- Find an *industrial designer* who is willing to spend one day sketching your idea – even if it is a simple, black-and - white perspective sketch.

- Find a *graphic designer* willing to spend one day on a mock up of your fake advertisement, with emphasis on the pain points you've identified. This ad should show your solution, feature a strong call to action, and include a good measure of surprise and delight. The sketch you got from your designer might work very well here. **Caution:** Do not show how you are solving the problem as it might start the "offered for sale patent timer."

- Find an *engineering company* willing to perform a one-day developmental strategy for your idea. At this point, it is OK to use ± estimates on tooling, material and labor.

- Find a *business development accountant* willing to spend one day with you, developing a business case prototype, again using wide range assumptions. This financial prototype should include first-year cost estimates, sales assumptions, breakeven, profit forecasts, and projected cash flow requirements.

- Find a reputable patent resource willing to quote a "not to exceed" search or who doesn't charge for an initial consultation.
- Kevin Prince at www.dirtcheappatents.com is a good example of a low cost patent search agent.
- Dan Girdwood at dlgirdwood@priceheneveld.com is a good example of a patent attorney who doesn't charge for initial counseling and understands you eventually will need to make your idea into a business before it can be successful.

- Find a *market research* company willing to do a one-day market search, looking for your idea.

- Spend a day at a trade show for the industry relevant to your product. Interview potential distributors, manufacturers, and partners. Be sure to show the problem, your idea for a solution, but NOT *how* you are doing it.

Most innovator groups look at prototyping only as a tool for developing the physical part. I say again, you MUST also prototype all phases of the business at the same time you are prototyping your part.

I have watched too many companies spend years getting the part perfect and, when a salesperson gets ready to start making sales calls, at the last minute they say "Oh yeah, we need a brochure or something!"

Why *not* prototype your marketing, distribution, manufacturing, and supply strategies at the same time as your product? Prototyping your business does not have to be expensive. Here are some reasonable beginning targets if you can find someone that works independently. Corporate business development people will not believe these numbers and spend a lot more (why I don't know, but they will).

1.	2 Hours of Market Research	$200
2.	4 Hours of Industrial Design	$400
3.	4 Hours of Engineering	$300
4.	3 Hours of Marketing	$300
5.	Quick Patent Search	$300
6.	½ day of financial forecasting	$250
7.	Test the Market	$400

Total Est. $1,700 - $2,200

At the end of a two or three day process, you will have a very rough version of a business case with all areas included:

- A solution-based form and function sketch

- A test advertisement that will show the problem and solution with a call to action

- An estimate of investment and return on that investment

- A factory cost estimate

- A quick look at patentability potential

- Validation showing if your idea has been in the market

- An indication if the market will pull or if you have to push

Doesn't spending $2,000 to prototype your entire business make more sense that starting out by filing for a $15,000 patent you might not need? Or why would you spend thousands on a perfect prototype that will change several times before you know if there is a market?

What the Heck is a Business FMEA?

Once you think that you might have a business starting to form, you should create a BFMEA (Business Failure Mode Effects Analysis). Use this as a tool to prove you understand there are things that can go wrong and you have a plan ready if things do go wrong.

Most engineers are trained to ask themselves what could go wrong with their product design, and if it does, what are we going to do about it. And if we do attempt improvements, what are the consequences to the business plan? " This is called a PFMEA. (Product Failure Mode Effects Analysis)

The chart shown as Fig 6 is a mockup of a Business FMEA. I suggest you create your own to give credibility to your business plan — and to you.

You will use your Business Failure Mode Effects Analysis for every phase of your business. Examples:

1. Most business cases will include a "SWOT" (Strengths, Weaknesses, Opportunities, and Threats) analysis. The BFMEA works great for the threats section because it shows the fixes and the effects of the fixes.

2. If you are raising money from a Venture Capital Organization, Bank, Angel Group, or other investor, they will want proof that you are not blinded by your own vision. They want you to be ready for things that might go wrong — and have contingencies. Many inventors and innovators think acknowledging potential problems is showing weakness — however if someone asks "What

could go wrong?" and you say *"Nothing"* – it can be a huge credibility hit for you.

3. Get your suppliers to be a part of your BFMEA issues that align with their areas. You can even ask them to contribute to building the list and taking their share of the risk.

4. If you list potential problems and you are not sure of the fix, or the fix might kill your business plan, you might want to take that as a red flag and stop until you get the solutions figured out.

5. This table is an example only. You will have to determine your own potential risks, then develop fixes and calculate the business plan effect.

Business Failure Mode Effect Analysis

- What could fail?
- What could be the Potential Cause?
- How are you going to fix it (Solution)?
- How is the fix going to Impact your Business Case?

Item	Potential Cause	Solution	Biz Case Impact
Distribution Channel Failure	Channel Conflict With Existing System	Change the Online Strategy	None
Customers do not like latch sound	Engineering Changes due to spring failure	Change Material to 304 Stainless	Add $0.03 to BOM
Low priority with Sales Group	Already Too Busy (overloaded)	Use Targeted Representatives	Add 3% to Factory Cost
Negative Competitive Surprise	Offshore Pricing	Buy and Use Automation Equipment	$23,000 capex or $0.23 cost per part
Margin Loss Due to Slow Inventory Turns	Custom Order Processing Speed	Hire Fulfillment House	Add $1.50 Cost Per Order

Figure 6

Story Time

Using BFMEA Planning 🐵🐵

Sometimes, when a vehicle is not selling well, it is a great time to be an accessory supplier to a car company — especially if you are fast at getting accessories ready to go into production.

A car company came to us and asked what we could do to improve the sales of a specific model by including features to match their competitor's better-selling car. They regarded their product as being in the same class.

It just so happened that we supplied their competitor with a freestanding floor console that incorporated a comfortable armrest. That accessory changed the feel for the driver. Long trips became less fatiguing and the car had a more upscale, cockpit feel.

The auto manufacturer's engineering and product planning groups were on-board, but the people with the money (purchasing) were dead set against it. With some hard selling, beautiful illustrations and prototypes, we got the order. One caveat was that we would have to amortize the tooling in the piece price and be willing to assume the entire cost for the tooling if the program was cancelled.

In other words, the only way we could get the order was to take all the risk. We did it but decided to include, in our Business Failure Mode Effects Analysis, the possibility that the car company's purchasing group might change their minds — and if so what we could do.

Before the Internet, car catalogues were the source of information for anyone looking to buy a new vehicle. These expensive and detailed catalogues were printed prior to the new model year launch. We provided the advertising agency with all of the photography and copy for this freestanding console. We did all of this without direct cost to our customers and their marketing people loved us for it.

Our BFMEA solution was to make cancellation almost impossible by following through on our delivery of these marketing support materials. Remember, these catalogues were printed in quantities of millions.

To make cancellation still harder, we hired a video production crew to shoot some B roll of the car showing the features and benefits our part. We supplied the footage to their preferred TV broadcast source which we knew would be a resource for national TV advertisements.

Now, if purchasing decided to cancel the part, they would have to scrap millions of printed catalogs and perhaps even some TV advertising.

Sure enough, one day I was in this customer's purchasing lobby when the buyer for this part got my attention. He said he had a new boss and he cancelled our part and wanted to see me immediately.

I went to his office where he was in a meeting with his direct reports. He had instructed his secretary that if I showed up, I was to come right into his meeting and interrupt. So I did.

This new VP of Purchasing for one of the largest car manufacturers in the world began to rant, rave, and use rude language. He told me that as long as he was with this company we would never get another new piece of business with them (for reasons that did not make sense).

I knew we had already implemented our Business FMEA plans and our part was already included and distributed to thousands of dealers around the world in several languages and, because of that, he could not cancel the part.

I said nothing because I did not want him to be embarrassed in front of his direct reports when I told this very emotional individual the lecture he just delivered was not going to happen.

At the end of his rant he said "any questions"? I apologized for whatever might have happened to cause him to be upset, but asked if I could have two minutes with him in private.

He agreed reluctantly. We went to another office where I told him that I would be happy to cancel the parts or move them to another supplier. I said we would do whatever we needed to do to fix this but there were a couple of issues on which we needed his help.

I told him about the printed catalogs and the upcoming TV advertising that specified our part as a new feature. I asked what he thought his group should do regarding pulling these catalogues and stopping the scheduled TV spots including the upcoming National Football League playoff spots.

To make a long story a little shorter, we kept the supply for this part and ran it for six years as well as expanded the usage into other vehicles. The purchasing VP and I eventually became friends and all went well for years after that shocking introduction.

The point is, when we have a doubt about a mechanical part we put an product PFMEA plan together. So why not do a BFMEA for your new business?

Finding and Spending Money

Finding money can be a daunting task. There are several ways to fund your ideas and business development.

I have been in many meetings, watching innovators pitch to funding sources. Most credible funding sources have excellent screening tools. All of the tools have adjustable risk tolerance, depending on the perceived risk/reward structure, and allowances for some missing pieces in the business plan.

The lenders dilemma is that most screening tools are designed to eliminate risk. But it gets complicated because the best returns possible for investors are usually at the beginning of an idea, precisely when there is the greatest risk.

The biggest mistakes I see when asking for money are:

1. Not having a plan to show where the money will be spent, with a backup plan if you run out

2. Giving up too much future equity in trade for money or services (engineering, design, tooling, etc.)

3. Not doing things like a BFMEA to show you have thought about what might go wrong and what you are going to do if that happens. It adds tremendous credibility. When someone asks a question about a new potential failure point, you can say, "That is a good question and we have not thought about that. Let us take a few days. We will add it to our BFMEA and get back to you." The alternative answer being, "We don't

think anything could possibly go wrong," which is best kept unsaid.

4. Spending too much on the non-value-added areas in the beginning (office, employees, etc.)

5. Borrowing from friends and family (potential red flag issue)

6. Spending on a patent when there is no evidence of a market. This is like buying a scratch off lottery ticket and you are so sure you have a winner you are spending money before you scratch off the cover. Find out if you have a winner before you spend the money!

7. Getting blinded by the dream of what you are going to do with the millions you are surely going to make and overselling to everyone you talk to. Recognizing overselling is easy for investors to do when they see the inventor focusing on the rewards their idea will provide him instead of why the market is going to reward all involved for providing great value.

8. Overspending with every developmental supplier by not providing clear plans and not using "not to exceed" agreements

9. Not bootstrapping (pay as you go) funding in the beginning to grow at a rate cash flow can cover versus starting with huge debt

A Grid of Funding Sources

There are all sorts of funding sources available. The diagram in figure 7 shows potential funding sources in a four-part grid. The two vectors are: how close you are to a sale and how much differentiation your product provides — including patent protection.

One of the most important things you can do to secure funding is to complete as many of the planning steps as you can in this book. There is an old axiom with which I do *NOT* agree — *"Invent a better mouse trap and the world will beat a path to your door."* I think it should say, *"Get a confirmed order for a unique, patented product, and money will not be an issue."*

If your idea is not unique and you have no idea how you are going to sell it, you will find yourself in the lower left quadrant of the grid below. This position will likely cause tension at the next family reunion. Or, you can borrow from the mob boss who does not care about risk because it is all yours.

Confirmed Sales	Short term (quick exit)	Bank (Cash Flow)
No Sales	Friends-Family-Fools	VC's and Angels
	No Patent	Patented

Figure 7

Story Time

Big Orders vs. Cash Flow

I was contacted by a large marketing firm that wanted to purchase $50,000 worth of products a month for six months. The product was to be used as a promotional tool. Because of the way I had to order parts, I would need almost $250,000 for cash flow.

I was not ready to take that risk. I told the company I would be glad to take the order, but they would have to pay me 50% up front and/or supply a letter of credit approved by my bank.

We could not come to agreement so I refused the order. This might sound crazy but these parts were going to be custom. All it would take is a new boss to change the buyer's mind and I would be holding a quarter of a million dollars worth of products I could not sell anywhere. My only alternative would be to spend $250,001.00 on lawyers to get $250,000.00 back.

Be careful when it comes to getting big orders – you might get more than you hoped for.

The Dilemma of Lenders Lag

Anytime an inventor, innovator, or entrepreneur needs funding, it is safe to assume they have a higher confidence level in the beginning of the project than probably anyone on earth.

Therefore, in the beginning, there is usually a gap in the understanding of risk levels between the inventors and potential investors. This is true if you work alone or work inside a company trying to get funding for your project.

I call this gap in recognizing risk levels "lenders lag," and in many ways it is like investing in the stock market. We all know it is better to invest during a market drop instead of a peak. But there can be a disconnect between what we know we should do versus what we want to risk. Investing in a new idea follows the same pattern. If investors place their bets early (when there is the most risk) they can likely strike a deal for better returns.

Visually, this looks like Figure 8, which shows some gap between the beginning (most risk) and when investors might be interested. This is not faulting the investor community. We would all want the same thing if we were investing in a startup business.

The other side of this is true also. If you cannot show evidence of value (page 13), you cannot expect to get top dollar for selling shares in a business concept. My point for writing about "Lenders Lag" is, we all know it exists in all deals, not as a good or bad thing but some level of it always exists.

The dilemma this brings up is that most investors want to wait to get involved until the risk can be quantified and get out when early signs of investment maturity show up. This makes sense for anyone thinking of investing in a new business.

Most innovators need to get financial support in the beginning when risk cannot be quantified to the point of satisfying investors or buyers. As stated earlier, make sure you need funding. But how can you know that until you test the market?

If you can launch your idea in a small way (a test market) to get sales and a good representation of positive feedback, you can demonstrate customer acceptance, and your ability to supply. This will demonstrate "evidence of value."

Also, if the inventor and the lender can openly identify the top five assumptions for stating the value and share proposals, instead of using "behind the scenes" tactics it can eliminate a lot of wasted time.

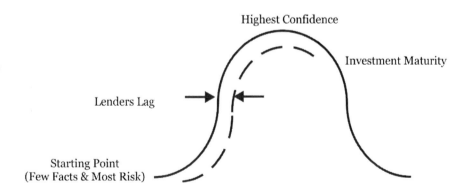

Demonstrating Market Evidence of Value can Reduce Lenders Lag

Figure 8

Story Time

Selling Your Idea Now or Later

As I write this book, a business partner and I have a new product on which we are about to be awarded a patent. We are well into the marketing and brand building process. Already, we have received interest from a few companies that might be interested in buying the business as is.

The problem is, with sales just getting started, it is hard for us to put a value on our company that would be acceptable to both parties. We can make assumptions using market testing and adjust that to fit their model, but in the end, it is hard to prove until there are long term sales.

One thing you can consider at this point is to look for a partner to share market expansion investments with well defined value splits for everyone involved. See Partners and Contracts on page 77. This gives the potential buyers and sellers a chance to test the relationship and business by looking at new opportunity together instead of immediately going to a buy/sell process.

A dilemma for potential buyers is that there will never be a cheaper time to buy our business. The dilemma for us is we have to continue to invest time and money to get initial sales so we can show the beginnings of a success curve.

In the end, it is best to get some sales and customer feedback so you can construct a future value forecast. You can use initial sales to build a best case, worst case, and most likely value curves. Using different success curves can shift the debate away from "will it" be successful to "which curve" fits the likelihood of success best.

Oh Yeah? What About YOU?

I often see entrepreneurs partnering with people who are clones of themselves. It seems to be the easiest way to get something done because everyone is thinking the same way. If you and your partner are the same pieces to your business puzzle, it could be a problem.

Complimentary fits are when one person wants to be out front of the business in the public eye and the other person wants to be behind the scenes running operations. If both people want to be the figurehead – get ready to go to alert levels orange and red because it is just a matter of time.

The big risk here is that two people with the same skills, the same preferences, and the same interests, might start a business because they hang out together and enjoy daydreaming about doing exactly the same things. Hey, I do it all the time with buddies – it is a hoot!

It is more effective to get some help where you need it and not just where it creates the most harmony. Narrow vision is not an asset.

It is hard to know why some people were born to think of new ways to do things or improve the way something has always been done. Inside companies, it is almost universal that the people who think of new things are not the same people who wrap a business around the idea.

Many inventors tend to be type B personalities — more at home in the lab than in the board room. I have no data on this; it is just my observation.

When you are working by yourself, it is really important to put a plan together that includes getting help in the areas that are not your strengths. If you are not comfortable with selling or making things, get someone who is.

Join invention groups, increase your network, and find a mentor. Attend industry shows and talk to others that have done what you are starting. I cannot overemphasize the importance of creating a community around your business.

Being the innovator or inventor can feel as if you are in the loneliest place in the world.

If you are working on your own, every time you ask someone to do something for you, if they don't show excitement, it can feel like they don't get it. Be careful here because it is a lot to expect that someone who has just heard your idea will immediately jump onboard.

If you are working for a corporation, it can feel as if you are working on an island.

I have been in both places many times. You feel you have a solution yet nobody cares. If you are a rookie, don't let this stop you. It can happen regardless of how many success stories you have in your resume.

You must show real patience with the people around you. When an idea is new, it is just that — an idea or a vision with no evidence of value (page 13). Most new visions have no factual evidence and it is easy to understand why other people might not grasp your vision the first time they hear about it.

In my earlier days, I would use all my energy and exhaust myself and almost everyone around me by doing whatever it took to convince others to get onboard.

About the time I turned forty, I discovered there was another way. I was watching a movie about a fighting style called Aikido. Aikido is performed by blending with the motion of the attacker and redirecting the force of the attack rather than opposing it head-on.

Another way of saying this came from the *Godfather* movies. I will modify the quote to say *"Keep your friends close but your devil's advocates closer."*

When someone comes to you with doubts or suggestions, be careful not to get defensive. Don't start pushing back and force everyone to take sides. In fact, thank the individual for offering to help and ask them what they suggest you do. This does not mean you necessarily do everything they are suggesting because there might be information you cannot or did not share. But you listen and seriously consider what they are saying.

There are several reasons for taking this approach of redirecting their energy. The first reason to listen is that they might be right. Second, it takes less effort for you to let their energy move you forward by adjusting their direction a little instead of trying to stop it and become exhausted (Aikido). The third reason is, you would be amazed how many supporters you will gain by asking for help instead of arguing your point.

Putting the Task in Perspective

Figure 9 is a modified example of a real business strategy I put together for a product I designed and launched a few years ago.

I have modified the names and activities maintain the anonymity of customers and partners. I am adding this to give you a perspective of the breadth of the task you are considering. This is sort of a visual business plan map that would make a great addendum to your business presentation package. The software I use is from *Mindjet*. It helps me visualize the activities I am planning around an idea. I am not saying you need to graphically map your business plan; I just want to show you the scope of what I plan **before** I move too far with product development.

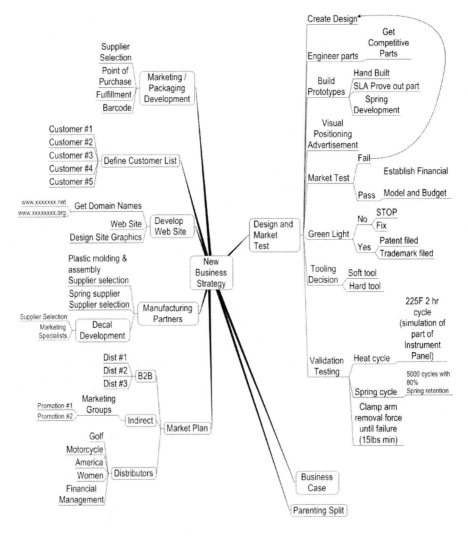

Figure 9

Managing Growth

If you have read this book, hopefully you have some new insight to what your growth teams go through on a daily basis.

I want to address this last section of the book to five groups:

1. Those of you who manage growth at companies and have earned your position by starting out as an inventor or innovator and grew into management.
2. Those that got to new business development management positions using other avenues — the conventional management track. My goal for you is to demonstrate what your innovators go through to get approvals.
3. Those executives who innovators approach for loans. My goal is to provide you some tools to read between the lines of the screening tools you use.
4. Those CEOs or Presidents of companies who and wonder what goes on with your growth groups – I hope this helps.
5. And, of course, those of you who are inventors or innovators. I hope I can give you some insight to what the people weighing your request for support are going through. As you read the rest of this book, put yourself in the shoes of the entrepreneurs you are trying to persuade.

Since I started my own company nine years ago, I continually find myself working with companies that struggle with getting their new product investment to pay off.

When I get a call from a CEO, I start by interviewing the leadership to find out why they think things are not going well.

I do this to find out if they are really committed to investing in the future, by determining if investing in growth is a "must have" or a "nice to have."

During these interviews I almost always find a number of common roadblocks. Here are just three examples:

1. **My Way or the Highway** - Upper management likes a specific idea and is blind to available alternatives. They look the other way when shortcuts are taken to get past traditional screening tools. They may refuse to consider anything which is NIH (Not Invented Here). If they did not think of the idea, it can't possibly be good. Most of the time, when this phenomenon is in play, everyone knows about it but can't talk about it – not even the board!

   This is a tricky area because the CEO still might be a fantastic inventor who was forced to learn to be a CEO by taking an idea from concept to success. It is not unusual to find these creative individuals running a large company at which he is just doing okay. But if he is a brilliant inventor and a mediocre CEO, which job does he do? Last I heard CEO pay is really good.

2. **The Sweetheart Team** If a group in the system has real or assumed new product success history, management tends to treat this group differently than other groups. The chosen group gets more ideas developed, more funding and management support. Other groups that may have game-changing ideas are forced to work within a system that has approval hurdles that are mainly in place to say no.

3. **The Renegade** - Some individuals in the company sell first, ignore the approval process and just get things done. Their working mantra is "it is easier to get forgiveness than permission." Management tolerates (or even celebrates) these people because they seem to be moving the company forward. *While the renegade can seem effective, many times he or she can steamroll other creative people who stay within the system to get approvals.*

I bring up these observations, not because they are right or wrong. If they work and become standard practice, just be prepared to accept the downside.

By denying the fact that the written rules do NOT match what is really being done, you sabotage continuous improvement in your new business development process. When exceptions become the rule, there is no system or at least it is out of control therefore guaranteeing incremental instead of breakthrough innovation.

On the other hand, the renegades may provide management with the answer to continuous improvement of the new business development process. If you know exactly how and why renegades and aggressive leaders bypass rules that slow down the people that play by the rules, you have access to key insights. When screening tools make approvals increasingly hard to get, renegades will find ways to work around the screens and produce winners. Wise management will adjust screening tools accordingly.

I find it interesting to look back and see who put together the approval process inside companies. Many times the people who put together these screening tools never developed a business on their own. But somehow, they have become experts on how to lower risk. They have figured out the best way to do that is to never say yes. After all, the only answer that eliminates risk is "no" which seems popular until sales fall off a cliff.

Many inventors, with whom I have worked, left companies with restrictive systems. They went on to create huge, successful businesses for which they developed systems that nurture idea generation — systems that, in their old companies, would never approve their ideas for funding.

On the other hand all of us know creative risk takers that started with a dream and ended up with very successful companies – it happens all the time. However, the ironic part of these "rags to riches" stories is that, at times, these same dreamers create new business approval systems that would never have approved their original idea. Then they wonder why there are no breakthrough ideas. Put simply – they lost their hunger and appetite for risk.

Here is a sample of the questions I ask when I work with a company that is wondering why they are not getting the bang for their new growth investment buck:

When you budget for new products, is it real money?

In your strategic plan, you might have a mandate to invest X% of pre-tax profits in new business growth, based on new products.

Do you have an executive in charge of spending that money whose bonus is affected by its success? Do you enforce it?

When end-of-year budget time comes, do you reward this leader for spending it? Or do you congratulate them for not spending it as you do for the rest of the budget leaders?

If you do not have someone that sits as an equal at the table with the executive group — someone who is measured on getting new growth investment to the market, you might not be serious about new growth. If you reward leadership when new growth investment dollars are **not** spent, why budget it in the first place?

How close are your new business development teams to your customers?

What if research into the existing needs of your customers is not a requirement of your new product development teams? What if they do not consult their own sales groups before spending millions on new products? Is that a practice you support?

As stated earlier, when your new product development is driven by your customers pain points, the need to sell ceases. However, if the only group that is close to your customers does not work with new business development teams, pain points are not going to be fed into your process. When you get too focused on inside innovation without customer pain point input, you can still have success, but not as much or as fast.

Are your salespeople held accountable for selling the new stuff?

When I talk to sales groups, I often separate them into two private rooms for a ten minute exercise. I ask one group to list the top five things their customers need to be successful that could be provided by their company. I ask the second group to list the top five things their own company needs to be successful. When I bring the two groups together to compare the lists, very seldom do any items match on the two lists. How can anyone justify running a company with a strategy that is not focused on their customers' success? Do you know what *your* sales groups would write on these two lists?

When I ask sales leaders why they think their new products continually miss the market, they often say "I could have told you that stuff would never sell – but nobody asked." How can it be okay for a sales group to not be held accountable for selling the newly developed products? Do they get a vote in how advanced investment dollars are spent? If not, shouldn't they?

Are your key products in the maturity phase of their business life cycle? 👥👥👥👥

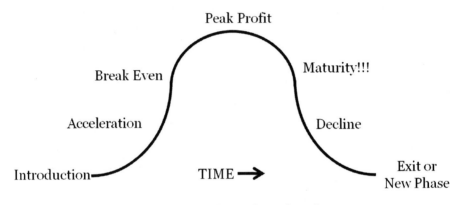

Product Life Cycle – All Products live this Curve

Figure 10

Figure 10 above is the same product life cycle chart we all learned about in marketing 101. All products experience this life cycle with one vector being *time* and the other being the *amplitude of success*. Some cycles last for 20 years and others just weeks or even days. The reason I point this out is that, by far, the one phase I see individuals and corporations ignore most often is the *maturity* phase.

Here are seven signals (and one suggestion) that your product is entering or may even be past the maturity phase:

1.   **You are lowering price and still losing market share**. But you are convinced your competition is giving their products away so they will be going broke soon and when they do, your pricing power will come back strong. *By the way this is NEVER true!*

2.   **New competition is popping up all the time**. The barriers of entry you once enjoyed are now more rumor than fact. Regardless of past success all products and business models have a life cycle. More frequent competition is a sure sign something is changing for the worse. Be careful here. It is not unusual for successful companies to go into "denial" when it comes to believing someone new can take their market share – even while they are watching it happen.

3.   **You are spending more money on lawyers protecting old products than you are on new businesses development**. By the way if you wait for your attorneys to stop this process you are going to be so broke, if it took a nickel to go around the world you could not get out of sight! And somebody will then sue you for your remaining nickel.

4.   **Your R&D money is not creating new business or there is no money for new products.** Your VP of operations keeps telling you to fire those crazy inventors and spend that money on that new time card system to catch those people staying on break too long. If you are the leader, and this sounds good because, "at least this can be measured," you are in desperate need of a vacation.

5.   Your budgeting process is playing more defense than offense. Yet, everyone is still getting bonuses, especially you and your CFO. Great while it lasts ...

6.   Key employees are leaving and the ones that stay are the same people that go along to get along.

The good news is that all these people leaving makes for a great quarter. The bad news is almost everything else.

Many by-the-book employees tend not to get involved with a new, risky idea if they do not see rewards for those who do take the risks to create growth.

The dilemma is that capable employees, who run toward the new ideas, might not use a written, official process. If they are successful, they might get rewarded on one hand but also reprimanded for not using the approved system. When this happens, the written system needs to change if the company wants to retain innovating leaders who are never satisfied with incremental growth.

7.   Are you missing key indicators that can predict that profit troubles may be ahead?

Often, in companies that ask for my help, when we do a little forensic profit research, we can see that profit deterioration did not happen overnight. As strange as this might sound, companies with the most success seem to be the first to ignore early signals that things are changing for the worse.

Hopefully, what we all went through in 2007 – 2009, served as a wakeup call. It would be impossible for me to list all the methods to predict profit troubles. An easy way would be to hire an extra pessimistic accounting staff, trained in Armageddon Accounting and pound them with energy drinks.

A better way might be to create red flag indicators that look for early margin erosion trends. A VP of Manufacturing I worked with years ago used to say, "It takes two data points to create a down-trend and at least seven to indicate an uptrend." At the time, I did not give that statement much thought. Now I think it has some merit. Run scared!

Many times, when companies ask me to help with more ideas, the last thing they need, is more ideas. Their process is like a clogged pipe. If someone stuffs more ideas into it, the backpressure would only get worse.

When it comes to converting more R&D money to profitable products, you unclog the pipe by cleaning up processes and eliminating the politics. By the way, when you try to eliminate the politics from a process, those that complain the loudest are the ones that have the most to lose – my guess would be turf!

Often, I can help companies find ways to clean this up to the point where a new business process feels like it is turbocharged and people are fighting to be a part of it.

But before there can be any change in the system, it takes awareness from the executive group that there might be an opportunity — and acceptance that things can improve. Second, it takes a set of fresh eyes, an outside person with nothing at stake, to examine the entire business development process and work with the team to get them excited about new product development again.

8. Think about developing a process for listening to ideas from outside your company.

Although I understand the reasons completely, I find it a huge mistake for companies to NOT take ideas from outside their organization. Of course, it is easier to ignore outside ideas from a legal and ego standpoint, but you need to get over that.

I compare this to some cellular phone and computer developers who use an open source strategy and invite in application developers and therefore have thousands more features than their competitors who do not invite ideas from outside developers.

Some companies are hiring a third-party business development screener, with no dog in the fight, to evaluate each incoming idea.

The screener does a quick evaluation and, if the idea does not apply, they simply write a "thanks but no thanks" letter. For the ideas that catch their eye, they package and route them to the proper inside person to execute a quick market test.

I understand rules of the past. Being an inside leader of business growth for over 20 years, we never took one idea from the outside. It is a new day; the potential risk of having to pay a royalty is no longer enough to ignore the value of fresh ideas from wherever you can get them. Those that argue otherwise have something to protect – turf!

A Checklist

This Checklist is for Inventors, Innovators, and Entrepreneurs who work alone or inside a company.

- Did you buy an inventor's notebook with numbered pages and a three-ring binder to hold your copies? Do you get others to witness important milestones? Witnesses should sign their name along with the date by your sketch or description of an idea.

- Did you search the markets, patents, and make copies of your work? Did you have it all verified with an outside source while creating a patent/competitive matrix? Did you buy all the relevant industry magazines, go to an industry show, and search for distributors?

- Did you create a test advertisement to get early feedback on your value story? Remember if you struggle with creating a simple advertisement that people immediately see "evidence of value" (page 13) you should consider this a Red Flag and stop until you can accomplish this.

- Did you develop a strategy to sell your idea to everyone from customers to investors and identify the pain points of every group you will be selling to?

- Did you develop a matrix to drive partnerships, joint ventures, and supply contracts?

- Did you create a strategy and budget for building a prototype of all phases of your business?

- Did you identify suppliers who are willing to add the one-day prototype to their service story?

- Did you create a business BFMEA (Business Failure Mode Effects Analysis) to use for all phases of your business development?

- Did you create a sales communication strategy? (see selling with evidence on page 73 and a better way to sell at home and away on page 58)

- Have you written a strategy for raising money that includes getting early customer feedback?

- Have you talked to your family about the sacrifice they will need to make if you go forward with your business plan?

- Did you write a business plan? There are dozens of good books available that can show you how to put together a business plan. Just go to any entrepreneurial section in your bookstore or search online and pick one up.

Summary

Starting a new business can be the hardest thing you will ever do but also can be the most rewarding. There are plenty of books and speakers who can tell you how to do each step. But before you buy a book or go to a seminar, make sure the author has actually launched a business and developed several products.

As you have seen, there is very little in this book on ideation and developing a product. This book focuses on one of the biggest challenges for us as inventors, innovators, and entrepreneurs, which is to stop looking at the opportunity as a "new product" and understand what you really need to do is create a new business based on the idea.

I want you to be sure your personality and life style are a fit for inventing and launching a new business based on your idea. I also want to save you time and money by testing your idea early in the process.

We have all heard that a person's greatest strength can also be their greatest weakness. For inventors, the greatest strength is their ability to think of new solutions. That strength can also be a liability when it comes to launching a new business. Just because someone can think of great solutions does not mean they have the ability and desire to manage a new business.

There is no shame in stopping a program when the time is right. In fact, I say celebrate the fact you stopped early and move on to the next idea.

In the beginning of this book I asked you three questions that I hope you can answer before you move forward with your idea. They are:

Are you an Inventor?

Are you an Innovator?

Are you an Entrepreneur?

After reading this book, I hope you know a little more about your own strengths and can apply them to your dreams and goals.

I also hope you have some idea about how to build a good cross-functional group with diversified talent, a group that is free to disagree without being disagreeable.

So, find some mentors and listen to them. Work at a brisk but comfortable pace. Never stop increasing the value of what you supply. Learn as you go.

If you are part of a corporate innovation team, hang in there and know that if you stay focused on helping your customers be successful and continue expanding your inside support team, you will do fine.

If you are a lone inventor, at times this might all seem like too much. That is okay, because one of my goals is to help you accept the fact if this business creation process does seem like too much, it is okay to take a break, get some help, or even stop before you create unmanageable debt.

Thinking up new products and solutions is a hobby of mine regardless of whether I move forward with a business. You can have that same hobby without moving forward with your ideas. Just get a kick out of your cleverness and keep your day job.

You don't need to use all of the tools I have provided. I am sure some will be more helpful than others. However, I promise that more tools you use the better your odds will be.

All of this starts with you giving yourself the freedom to dream. Every bit of human progress, since the beginning of time, started with a dream (or vision if you like). Without a dream, nothing is feasible or even possible. A great way to start is by gathering "evidence of value" which is where the work starts and I hope this book gives you some perspective on what that journey might be like.

But most importantly – have fun! If it is not fun, go find something that is and enjoy the time you have on this earth doing something you love!

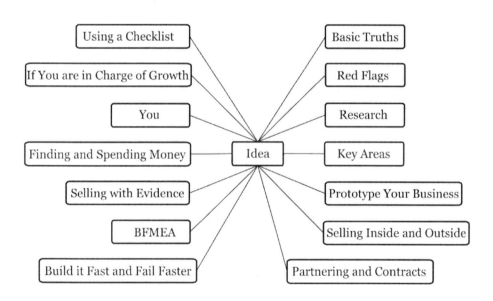

You did it! Thanks for sharing your time with me, now go make something happen.

Index

About The Author

I have always been curious about technology. At age ten, I dismantled a light bulb because I was wondering how it worked. I learned the hard way that a light bulb filament is like a flash bulb without the glass envelope – goodbye facial hair!

I was very interested in school when the subjects were things that I liked, and found it hard to pay attention otherwise. I took longer to get an undergraduate degree than most college students, although I have never stopped taking classes and formally learning at some level while still plodding toward my masters.

Jobs have always been an important part of my learning process, from cutting meat and delivering fuel to farmers in high school to owning my own development company. I've never keep track of the hours I work especially if I am on a team, creating a new product and business.

I started out working for General Motors and then became a Vice President for Prince Corporation, which was a highly innovative company in Holland, Michigan. When I started at Prince, our sales were about twenty million dollars a year. When the founder (who was a really cool guy) passed away and the company was sold to Johnson Controls Automotive Division, Prince Corporation sales were approaching one billion dollars a year.

I was promoted to Group Vice President for Johnson Controls Automotive, which at the time was a twenty billion dollar division of JCI. At both companies I managed new business development, marketing and advanced sales. At JCI we added things like PR, IT and working with the financial analysts.

I have had the good fortune to work with many great teams and this week I am filing for my 50th patent, all of which would have no value if they did not create profit.

I enjoy speaking to and working with companies that have growth or profit challenges by helping examine and refocus their business growth engines.

I also enjoy creating a business around any idea to give it the best chance it can possibly have.